D1125573

25 BICYCLE TOURS
in Maryland

Other books by Anne H. Oman

25 Bicycle Tours in and around Washington, D.C.
Saturday's Child: Family Activities in Metropolitan Washington

25

BICYCLE TOURS
in Maryland

From the Allegheny Mountains to the Chesapeake Bay

Anne H. Oman

With photographs by the author

SECOND EDITION

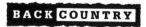
Backcountry Guides
Woodstock · Vermont

An invitation to the reader

Although it is unlikely that the roads you cycle on these tours will change much with time, some road signs, landmarks, and other items may. If you find that such changes have occurred on these routes, please let the author and publisher know, so that corrections may be made in future editions. Other comments and suggestions are also welcome. Address all correspondence to:

Editor, 25 Bicycle Tours series
The Countryman Press
P.O. Box 748
Woodstock, Vermont 05091

Library of Congress Cataloging-in-Publication Data

Oman, Anne H.
  25 bicycle tours in Maryland : from the Allegheny Mountains to Chesapeake Bay ; with photographs by the author / Anne H. Oman—2nd ed.
      p. cm.
  ISBN 10-digit: 0-88150-495-5
  ISBN 13-digit: 978-0-88150-495-8
  1. Bicycle touring—Maryland—Guidebooks. 2. Bicycle trails—Maryland—Guidebooks. 3. Maryland—Guidebooks. I. Title: Twenty five bicycle tours in Maryland. II. Title.

GV1045.5.M3 O43 2001
917.5204'44—dc21   2001037529

Copyright © 1994, 2001 by Anne H. Oman

Second Edition

All rights reserved. No part of this book may be reproduced in any form, or by any electronic or mechanical means, including information storage and retrieval systems, without permission in writing from the publisher, except by a reviewer, who may quote brief passages.

Cover design by Bodenweber Design
Cover and interior photographs by Anne H. Oman
Interior design by Sally Sherman
Maps by Richard Widhu, © 2001 The Countryman Press

Published by The Countryman Press,
P.O. Box 748, Woodstock, Vermont, 05091
Distributed by W.W. Norton & Company, Inc.,
500 Fifth Avenue, New York, NY 10110
Printed in the United States of America
10 9 8 7 6 5 4 3

Acknowledgments

I'd like to thank the following people who rode with me in a dauntless quest for truth, or at least, accuracy: Ralph Oman, Tabitha Oman, Caroline Oman, Charlotte Oman, Betsy Agle, Dwayne Poston, Nancy Martin, Summer Martin, Diana Cadeddu, Mark Joelson, Tato Joelson, Nancy Renfrow, Charlie Borden, Tina Borden, Gary Ferraro, Kathryn Ferraro, Jessica Frank, Joslin Frank, Matt Erskine, Ann Webber, Mike Remington, Elise Remington, Christophe Remington, Lorna Ferguson, and Terry Clark.

*This book is dedicated
with love and gratitude to Ralph Oman,
who fixed flats, loaded the bike rack,
read maps, and did on-the-spot repairs.*

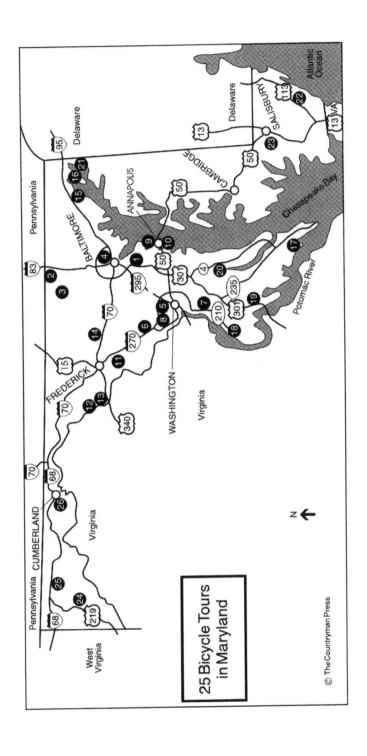

25 Bicycle Tours
in Maryland

© The Countryman Press

Contents

GREATER BALTIMORE

GREATER WASHINGTON

ANNAPOLIS AREA

GREATER FREDERICK AREA

Publisher's Notice

Cycling involves inherent risks, and readers planning to follow tours in this book should first read carefully the "safety" section of the introduction. Cyclists in urban areas should also be alert to the problem of crime. Tours in this book are in areas considered safe to ride in at the time of publication, but cyclists should follow sensible precautions (such as never cycling at night and traveling with one or more companions) and should be alert to changing patterns of crime in the city.

25 Bicycle Tours at a Glance

Distance (miles)	Terrain	Highlights
13.5/18.5	Flat; some hills	Woods, wetlands, and crabs
14.6/21.7	Flat	Smooth riding along a rushing river
13.2	Hilly	Hills, but ice cream and a swim, too
9.8	Mostly flat	A city ride with stops for attractions
12.9	Mostly flat	A network of trails
13.2	Flat to rolling	Literary graves; eccentric architecture
16.6	Moderately hilly	History on the Potomac
6.2	Flat; some hills	A sylvan trail between suburbs
64.5	Moderately hilly	Middies, seafood, and history
5.2	Flat to rolling	Waterfowl and river views
19.2	Hilly	Country roads and water lilies
21.2	Flat and rolling	Civil War washed down with wine
27.2	Moderately hilly	Burnside Bridge to John Brown's raid
23.0	Moderately hilly	Visits to the wineries
17.8	Hilly	Charming Havre de Grace
27.7	Very hilly	To the lighthouse!
26.5	Flat; a few hills	17th- and 18th-century Maryland
26.5	Rolling	Churches and herons
23.7	Rolling	The escape route of Lincoln's killer
33.6	Hilly	Tobacco farms; antiques; the Chesapeake
45.0	Flat to rolling	An old canal town
94.9	Flat	Wild ponies and cultivated inns
34.7	Flat	Ferry rides and a river plantation
33.9	Very hilly	Lake, swamp, and waterfalls
15.5	Very hilly	Mountain roads and artisans
189.0	Flat; some hills	A swath through Maryland's history

Introduction to the Second Edition

From the Atlantic coastal plain to the forested peaks of the Appalachians, Maryland offers not only incredibly varied terrain but also a journey through history. The tours in this book will enable cyclists to sample Maryland's geography—from the Mason-Dixon line to the salt-marsh grazing grounds of the wild ponies of Assateague Island, from the West Virginia border to the Chesapeake Bay. They will also introduce cyclists to the panoply of Maryland's history, from the landing of the first white settlers to the graves of Revolutionary War soldiers, to forts used in the War of 1812, to Civil War battlefields, to early industrial sites, to twenty-first-century cities and suburbs, and to places where the timeless rhythm of agricultural pursuits still rules. On these tours, you can visit museums, old mills, lighthouses, wineries, crab houses, country inns, swimming places, the restaurants of Baltimore's Little Italy, the U.S. Naval Academy, Lily Pons Water Gardens, historic churches and homes, canal lock-houses, and spectacular waterfalls, among other attractions. A special feature of this edition is a trip along the length of the historic C&O Canal, which spans Maryland both geographically and historically.

So, get on your bike and enjoy the riches of Maryland.

About the Rides

The tours in this book vary not only in terrain, but also in length—from 5 to 95 miles. Some use off-road trails, shared with hikers and horses, while others use roads shared with cars. Trails and light-traffic roads are preferred, especially if you have children in your party. An attempt has been made to avoid roads with heavy traffic, but this was impossible in a few cases.

Because different cyclists set different paces, I haven't tried to estimate the time necessary to complete a tour. Even inexperienced cyclists can usually average about 12 miles per hour while actually cycling, but if you like to stop often to rest, eat, or sightsee, the hourly average will drop to about 5 miles. By that rule of thumb, a 40-mile trip will take about eight hours. For some tours, accommodations along the route are listed.

The tours are organized according to their proximity to four cities—Baltimore; Washington, DC; Annapolis; and Frederick—and, otherwise, according to broad geographical areas: the Eastern Shore, southern Maryland, northeast Maryland, and western Maryland.

Rules of the Road

Bicycles are prohibited on expressways and other controlled-access highways as well as on toll facilities such as bridges and tunnels. On other highways where the posted speed is more than 50 miles per hour, bicycles are banned from the travel lanes and must ride on the shoulder, even if the shoulder is unpaved. Along any other highways, cyclists must use the shoulder or bike lane if it is paved.

On all roads where bicycling is allowed, the operator must:
- Obey all traffic signals and signs
- Ride with the traffic as near to the right of the road or shoulder as possible
- Use standard hand signals
- Yield to pedestrians
- Move to the right or stop for emergency vehicles
- Stop for loading and unloading of school buses when warning lights are flashing
- Obey all applicable traffic laws, such as the prohibition of passing on the right

Bicycles must be equipped with:
- Brakes that make the braked wheel skid on dry, clean pavement
- A bell or horn
- A rear red reflector
- A white-beam headlight (if ridden at night)

In addition, the Maryland Department of Transportation strongly encourages the use of a bicycle helmet, rearview mirror, and red taillight.

Resources

The Maryland State Highway Administration has a Bicycle Affairs Coordinator, who performs research and monitors state highway projects for bicycle compatibility. This office offers a number of free brochures on

A cyclist pauses to read the map on the 184-mile C&O Canal towpath, which traverses Maryland from the mountains to the tidewater.

bicycle safety, regulations, ferry service, and trails. For information write to Bicycle Affairs Coordinator, Room 218, Maryland State Highway Administration, 707 North Calvert Street, Baltimore, MD 21202, or call 1-800-252-8776.

The state also operates a bicycle information hot line, 1-800-252-8776, which is staffed from 8:30 AM to 4:30 PM weekdays. By calling this number and leaving your name and mailing address, you can also request a packet of free bicycling information.

The Department of Economic and Employment Development has published a color-coded *Maryland Bicycle Touring Map*. It is available free from the Office of Tourism Development, 217 East Redwood Street, Baltimore, MD 21202, 1-800-543-1036.

About Safety

Cycling involves two kinds of safety considerations: safety from possible criminal activity as well as from traffic hazards. The tours in this book are all in areas considered safe, in daylight hours, at the time of publication. But "safe" is a relative term, and no place is completely without danger. Prudent cyclists will use common sense to protect themselves and their bikes against crime and other dangers. In addition to complying with the state laws concerning cycling (see "Rules of the Road"), the following guidelines should be used:

- Never ride alone, particularly on a secluded trail or road.
- Always let someone know what route you are taking.
- Don't ride after dark.
- Carry a whistle around your neck or an air horn in an accessible pocket. Noise can both bring help and scare away attackers.
- When riding with companions, ride single file at least 20 feet apart.
- Don't wear headsets or earplugs.
- Be sure your bicycle is in good working order.
- Watch out for storm drains, potholes, railroad or trolley tracks, patches of sand or gravel, and other road hazards.
- Ride defensively. Expect the unexpected—such as a parked car's door opening in front of your path.
- Pull well away from the road when you stop to rest or check the map.

Bike Security

Always secure your bike when you leave it—even if it's for a few minutes. This is especially important in urban areas, where bicycle theft is a serious problem. The kind of lock most likely to foil bicycle thieves is the U-shaped shackle lock, sold under such brand names as Kryptonite and Citadel. These are expensive, but not as expensive as a new bicycle. And police departments in some jurisdictions report that bicycle thefts have actually declined since these locks were introduced in the 1970s. Here are some additional security tips:

- Lock your bike to something permanent and in a place where any attempted theft is likely to be noticed.
- Lock up as much of your bike as possible. If you have quick-release wheels, remove the front wheel and put the lock through the front wheel, the rear wheel, and the frame, securing it to the rack, tree, or other fixture. Remove any accessories you don't want to lose—pumps, water bottles, and computer-type odometers are vulnerable to theft.
- Register your bike with the local police department. This will greatly enhance your chances of getting it back if it's stolen.

About Equipment

In addition to the equipment required or recommended by the Maryland Department of Transportation (see "Rules of the Road"), you should carry a patch kit, a spare tube, and an air pump. An odometer is handy for gauging distance, although you should be able to follow the directions in this book without one.

Rentals

Many bicycle shops rent bikes, racks, child carriers, helmets, and other equipment. At the end of each tour in this book, at least one bicycle shop is listed. Those that rent bikes are indicated. It's best to reserve the equipment you want in advance.

About Metrorail

Four of the tours in this book (tour 5, A Branch Water Tour; tour 6, "So We Beat On . . ."; tour 8, Inter-Suburb Sprint; and tour 9, Capital-to-Capital Express) suggest using Metrorail (also known as Metro) as an alternative way of getting to and from the starting point. The Washington Metropolitan Area Transit Authority allows bicyclists to bring their bikes on the trains anytime except 7 AM to 10 AM and 4 PM to 7 PM on weekdays. Permits are no longer required. Use the elevator entrance and read the rules posted inside the elevator. For more information and to make sure these rules are still operative, call 202-962-1116. If you don't want to use Metrorail, the stations used as starting points in the tours involved have parking lots, which are free on weekends.

Bicycle Clubs

The Maryland Department of Transportation lists the following recreational cycling clubs:
Annapolis Bicycle Club, P.O. Box 224, Annapolis, MD 21404
Appalachian Bicycle Club, P.O. Box 1254, Cumberland, MD 21502
Baltimore Bicycling Club, P.O. Box 5906, Baltimore, MD 21208
Cumberland Valley Cycling Club, P.O. Box 711, Hagerstown, MD 21740
Frederick Pedalers, P.O. Box 1293, Frederick, MD 21701
Freestate Derailleurs, 4424 MacWorth Place, Baltimore, MD 21236
Oxon Hill Bicycle and Trail Club, P.O. Box 81, Oxon Hill, MD 20745
Patuxent Area Cycling Enthusiasts, P.O. Box 1318, Solomons, MD 20688
Potomac Pedalers Touring Club, P.O. Box 23601, L'Enfant Plaza Station, Washington, DC 20026
Salisbury Bicycle Club, 708 Walnut Street, Pocomoke City, MD 21851

Cycle Across Maryland (CAM)

Every summer, usually toward the end of July, hundreds of cycling enthusiasts of widely varying abilities pedal across the state, or a good part of it. The route changes from year to year, and the trip usually takes four or five days. Participants pay a fee and stay at campgrounds, in facilities such as schools, or in motels and guest houses. The event is widely publicized through bicycle shops and newspapers, and the state Bicycle Coordinator can also provide information.

GREATER
BALTIMORE

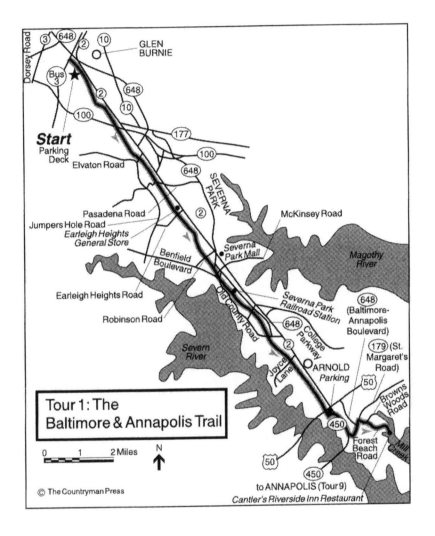

Tour 1: The
Baltimore & Annapolis Trail

0   1   2 Miles

N

© The Countryman Press

1

The Baltimore & Annapolis Trail

Location: Anne Arundel County
Terrain: Flat on bike trail, some hills on extension
Road conditions: Paved trail and paved roads
Distance: 13.3 miles on the trail, 18.5 miles if you continue to the restaurant
Highlights: Woods, wetlands, the Earleigh Heights General Store, the Severna Park Railroad Station, Cantler's Riverside Inn Restaurant

The Baltimore & Annapolis Trail Park, associated with the Rails to Trails Conservancy, follows the track bed of the defunct Baltimore & Annapolis Railroad from its northern terminus in Glen Burnie, a Baltimore suburb, to Annapolis, Maryland's seagoing capital. The 10-foot-wide path traverses a variety of landscapes—exurban shopping malls, small cities, backyards, and wildlife habitats. The trail ends across the Severn River from historic Annapolis, but the tour continues on country and suburban roads to a popular crab house on Mill Creek. The trail begins in Glen Burnie, on Dorsey Road just east of MD 3, and there is a parking lot.

0.0 From the parking lot, head south on the trail.

0.5 The trail leads through downtown Glen Burnie and crosses MD 3.

3.0 After crossing MD 100 on a bridge, the trail winds downhill.

4.3 At the intersection with Jumpers Hole Road are picnic tables, a gazebo, and a food store.

4.6 The trail runs through a wetland, then into some woods replete with wild dogwood and ferns.

6.3 The Earleigh Heights General Store, circa 1890, now houses an information center and rest rooms.

A liquor store across the trail sells sodas and snacks.

9.0 *The restored Severna Park Railroad Station was built in 1919.* In an exhibit case is a picture of the last train to run on this line, in 1950. In the surrounding center of this upscale suburb are an antiques shop and a shopping mall with an ice cream store.

10.3 *The final stretch of the trail passes through suburban Arnold's heavily shaded backyards.*

13.3 *After crossing under US 50, the off-road trail ends. Continue on a marked side-of-the-road path along Boulter's Way to the parking lot, which is at the intersection with MD 450.*

14.0 *If you want to continue the tour, turn right on MD 450 from the parking lot and ride on the paved shoulder.*

15.6 *Cross the highway—carefully—and climb some steps to a scenic overlook with a view of the Naval Academy, the State-house, and Annapolis Harbor.*

15.9 *At the light, MD 450 crosses the Severn into downtown Annapolis (see tour 9). This tour turns left on Baltimore-Annapolis Boulevard (MD 648) and travels through a posh residential section.*

17.0 *Turn right on St. Margaret's Road (MD 179).*

17.3 *At the fork marked by Sandy's Country Store, bear right on Browns Wood Road, which climbs a small hill.*

17.5 *Turn right on Forest Beach Road.*

18.5 *The road dead-ends at Cantler's Riverside Inn Restaurant, where you can end your trip with excellent crabs or other food and a view of Mill Creek.*

Bicycle Repair Services

Bike Doctor, Inc., 953 Ritchie Highway, Arnold; 410-544-3532
   No rentals
The Bike Pedalers, 5 Central Avenue, Glen Burnie; 410-761-7675
   Rentals

2
North Central Railroad Trail

Location: *Baltimore County*
Terrain: *Flat*
Road conditions: *Crushed-stone hiker-biker trail*
Distance: *14.6 miles (or 21.7 miles)*
Highlights: *Picturesque small towns and farms, Little Falls, the Gunpowder River, the Monkton railroad station*

To deliver his address at the site of the battle of Gettysburg, Lincoln traveled on the North Central Railroad; after his assassination, his body was taken west along these same tracks. Union soldiers were also transported on this line. Built in 1838 to carry flour, paper, milk, farm products, coal, and mail between such settlements as White Hall, Parkton, and Bentley Springs and the city of Baltimore, the North Central gradually gave way to truck transport. In 1972 Hurricane Agnes delivered the death blow, washing out bridges. In 1984 the tracks were removed and replaced by a recreational-use trail.

The trail extends from Ashland north to the Pennsylvania state line. This tour covers the northern two-thirds of the trail, which is pretty and not heavily traveled. It begins at the Freeland parking lot (2 miles west of MD 45 on Freeland Road), takes a short detour to the north end of the trail at the Mason-Dixon line, and then travels down the trail to the preserved turn-of-the-twentieth-century railroad station at Monkton.

0.0 *From the Freeland parking lot, turn left past the rest rooms and follow the trail north, up a slight grade, past farmhouses and through woods.*

Watch for horse piles and hikers, as this is a multiuse trail.

1.5 *The trail ends at the Pennsylvania border, or Mason-Dixon line.*

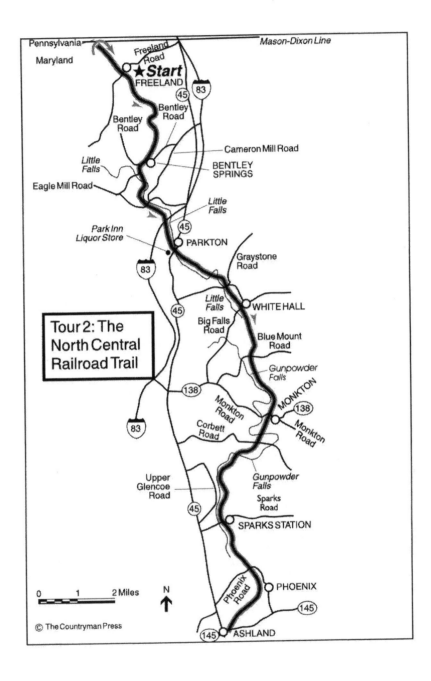

Tour 2: The North Central Railroad Trail

Plans to extend the trail into Pennsylvania are awaiting funding. The trip back down the trail affords a pleasant downhill glide. Return to the Freeland parking lot.

3.0 *Across a stream from the Freeland parking lot (right), the Flower Cafe sells snacks and shaved ice.*

Chairs and tables along the stream offer a respite. Continuing south on the trail, you'll pass Victorian homes with rocking chairs, which once afforded residents a view of the passing trains.

3.2 *As you cross the stream, look at the remains of the railroad tracks to your right.*

This part of the trail winds through woods. Roads cross at intervals, so observe stop signs.

6.3 *The trail crosses Little Falls, which is not actually a falls but a popular canoeing river.*

8.7 *The brick building to your left, now a private home, was once an inn for travelers. For refreshments turn right for 0.1 mile, following the sign that advertises pit beef.*

On weekends, a family sells barbecued beef in front of the Park Inn liquor store. Soda machines are available when the liquor store is closed, on Sunday.

8.9 *After this detour, turn right and continue south on the trail.*

Paths through the woods lead down to Little Falls, whose waters form inviting pools around boulders. Ferns line the banks of both stream and trail, creating a green glade.

11.0 *An antiques store to your left lures cyclists from the trail in the village of White Hall.*

Cows and horses graze in the field next to the store.

11.1 *The neoclassical White Hall National Bank dates from 1909.*

Just past White Hall, the trail runs along Gunpowder Falls, a popular tubing course.

14.6 *The Monkton railroad station, circa 1898, now houses a small museum and shop.*

Rest rooms are available here. Across the parking lot, which gets crowded on weekends, the Monkton General Store sells sand-

The restored Monkton station on the North Central Railroad Trail houses a small museum about the railroad.

wiches, drinks, and shaved ice. Additional parking lots south of Monkton are at Sparks (on Sparks Road east from MD 45), at Phoenix (on Phoenix Road east from MD 45), and at Ashland (on Ashland Road east from MD 45).

Bicycle Repair Service

Monkton Bike Rental, 1900 Monkton Road, Monkton; 410-771-4058
  Bikes, baby trailers, tubes, and canoes for rent
Adventure Bicycle Company, 3427 Sweet Air Road, Phoenix; 410-666-2453
  No rentals

3

The Hills of Hampstead

Location: *Carroll County*
Terrain: *Hilly*
Road conditions: *Paved country roads with light traffic*
Distance: *13.2 miles*
Highlights: *The country towns of Hampstead and Snydersburg,
    Simmons Home Made Ice Cream Store, Cascade Lake*

Carroll County consists mainly of hilly farm country that hugs the Maryland-Pennsylvania line. Originally settled by people of English stock, the area soon saw an influx of German-speaking farmers from nearby Pennsylvania. Although the suburban sprawl of greater Baltimore is making inroads, the county is still, by and large, rural. This tour loops through a corner of northeastern Carroll County, starting at North Carroll High School on MD 482 in Hampstead. After passing through the old-fashioned, front-porch town, it goes through farm country where cornfields and barns seem to be making a valiant stand against subdivisions. After a stop at an old-fashioned ice-cream store and a swim in a lake, the tour returns to Hampstead.

0.0 *Leaving the parking lot of North Carroll High School, turn
    right on MD 482.*

0.4 *Turn right on Main Street (MD 30).*

Hampstead is a typical northern Maryland town, with rockers and geraniums on the front porches and flags flying even when it's not a holiday.

1.3 *Turn right on Houcksville Road.*

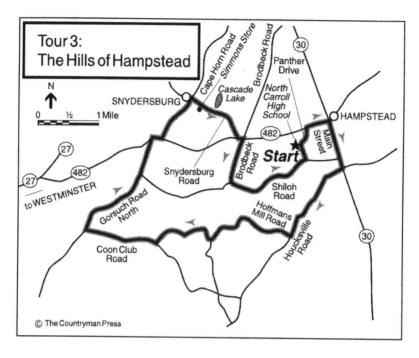

Tour 3:
The Hills of Hampstead

2.7 Turn right on Hoffmans Mill Road, a pretty country byway that runs through woods along a stream.

5.3 Turn right on Coon Club Road, which leads up a long hill and into a suburban area.

6.5 Turn right on Gorsuch Road North, which leads down one long hill and then, unfortunately, up another one.

8.1 Tall trees shade a rural graveyard to your left.

8.7 At the intersection with MD 482, turn right. Then make an immediate left onto Cape Horn Road.

9.5 In the village of Snydersburg, turn right on Snydersburg Road, in front of St. Mark's Lutheran Church Parsonage.

9.7 Simmons Store, to your right, has a little of everything, including hand-dipped ice-cream cones.

Cascade Lake, nestled in the hills of Hampstead, invites the cyclist to take a refreshing dip.

9.8 *Cascade Lake, to your left, a spring-fed, 6-acre natural lake, provides a good place for a refreshing swim in season.*

Admission is charged, and there are changing rooms, a pleasant snack bar overlooking the lake, floats to swim to, and boats to rent.

10.5 *Turn left on MD 482, then make an immediate right onto Brodbeck Road.*

11.3 *Turn left on Shiloh Road, a hilly, partly wooded road.*

12.7 *To your left is Shiloh Antiques.*

12.8 *Turn left on Panther Drive (unmarked), which leads onto the high school grounds.*

13.2 *Return to the North Carroll High School parking lot.*

Bicycle Repair Services

White's Bicycle, 12 West Main Street, Westminster; 410-848-3440
  No rentals

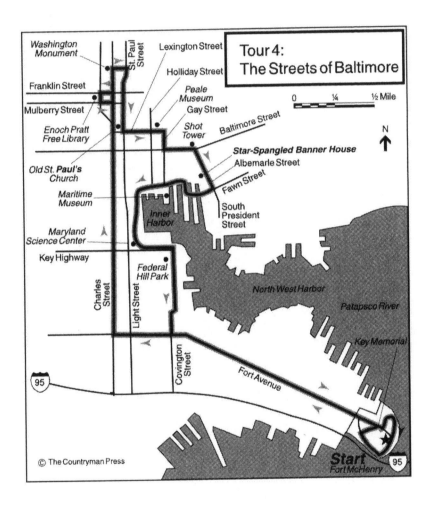

Tour 4:
The Streets of Baltimore

Washington Monument
St. Paul Street
Lexington Street
Holliday Street
Franklin Street
Peale Museum
Mulberry Street
Gay Street
Enoch Pratt Free Library
Shot Tower
Baltimore Street
0   ¼   ½ Mile
N
Star-Spangled Banner House
Old St. Paul's Church
Albemarle Street
Fawn Street
Maritime Museum
Inner Harbor
South President Street
Maryland Science Center
Key Highway
Charles Street
Light Street
Federal Hill Park
North West Harbor
Patapsco River
Covington Street
Key Memorial
95
Fort Avenue
© The Countryman Press
Start
Fort McHenry
95

4
The Streets of Baltimore

Location: *Baltimore City*
Terrain: *Mostly flat*
Road conditions: *City streets with light traffic on weekends*
Distance: *9.8 miles*
Highlights: *Fort McHenry, the Enoch Pratt Free Library, the Washington Monument, the Peale Museum, the Shot Tower, the Star-Spangled Banner House, Little Italy, the Inner Harbor*

The state song "My Maryland" exhorts Marylanders to "avenge the patriotic gore/that flecks the streets of Baltimore," referring to an incident that took place just after the outbreak of the Civil War. On April 19, 1861, 15 people were killed in a riot that broke out in this city of divided loyalties when a Massachusetts regiment was moved across town from one railroad station to another.

This tour leads bicyclists through those now-peaceful streets to attractions patriotic, literary, artistic, historic, religious, scientific, and gastronomic. It begins at the quintessential patriotic place—the fort that inspired a young lawyer named Francis Scott Key to write "The Star-Spangled Banner" during the War of 1812—and makes its way to Mount Vernon Place, site of the Walters Art Gallery, the Peabody Conservatory of Music, and the first monument to honor George Washington. After a stop at the city history museum and visits to the Shot Tower and to the house where the flag that flew over Fort McHenry was sewn, the tour threads through Little Italy, where only the strong can resist stopping at a restaurant. Baltimore's popular Inner Harbor, with a heady variety of museum, shopping, and food attractions, is the last stop before returning to Fort McHenry.

Fort McHenry may be reached from I-95, exit 55.

0.0 *From the parking lot next to the visitors center, turn right on the multipurpose trail along the Patapsco River.*

The truce ship from which Francis Scott Key saw the huge flag flying over Fort McHenry sat at anchor on the horizon, to your left.

0.2 *Lock your bike to a bench and visit the fort.*

Here valiant fighting in September 1814 sent the British fleet packing—first to Jamaica and then to New Orleans, where they finally lost the war.

There are frequent interpretative programs, and the visitors center provides an excellent film about the Battle of Baltimore.

0.6 *At the V, take the path on the right to a neoclassical statue honoring Francis Scott Key. Continue to the park entry road and turn left.*

Actually, the statue depicts Orpheus, the Greek god of music. When the statue was unveiled in 1922, President Warren G. Harding spoke, giving the first presidential speech broadcast on coast-to-coast radio.

1.0 *Exit the park and proceed straight ahead on Fort Avenue.*

This road crosses a railroad bridge; passes an interesting, vine-covered warehouse to your right; and travels through a traditional Baltimore blue-collar neighborhood with union halls and Permastone houses—some with marble stoops.

2.8 *Turn right on South Charles Street, which leads through the gentrified Federal Hill district, past several antiques shops, and into the downtown financial district.*

4.1 *To your right is Old St. Paul's.*

This basilica-style church was built in 1856 to serve a parish established in 1692. The architect, Richard Upjohn, also designed Trinity Church in New York City.

4.3 *Turn left on Franklin Street for 1 block.*

4.4 *Make another left on Cathedral Street.*

The neoclassical Enoch Pratt Free Library houses collected papers of two distinguished literary sons of Baltimore: H. L. Mencken and Edgar Allan Poe. Across the street stands the Basilica of the

Baltimore's Inner Harbor, once a drab industrial port, now draws visitors with its restaurants, museums, an aquarium, shops, and historic ships.

Assumption of the Blessed Virgin Mary, built between 1806 and 1821, the first Roman Catholic cathedral in the United States.

4.5 *Turn left on Mulberry Street.*

4.6 *Turn left on Charles Street.*

This street swoops down a hill and up another to the 164-foot Doric column topped by a 16-foot statue of George Washington.

To the left of the monument, across Charles Street, stands the Walters Art Gallery, with superb collections of classical, medieval, Renaissance, and Oriental art. To the right of the monument is the renowned Peabody Conservatory of Music, facing Mount Vernon Square, which could pass as the setting for a Masterpiece Theater series. Cross the square and turn right, in front of the Victorian gothic Mount Vernon Place Methodist Church, heading downhill on cobblestoned Mount Vernon Place.

4.9 *Turn right on St. Paul Street.*

Stop to admire the statue of Severn Teacke Wallis, a lawyer, poet, and ancestor of Wallis Warfield, the Baltimore girl who eventually became the Duchess of Windsor.

5.4 *Turn left on Lexington Street.*

5.5 *Turn left on Holliday Street to the Municipal Museum of the City of Baltimore, also called the Peale Museum, to your right.*

This museum, opened in 1814 by the artist brothers Rembrandt and Rubens Peale, was America's first museum. It featured paintings by the gallery owners and their father, Charles Wilson Peale, renowned portraitist of George Washington. It also included a "cabinet of natural history." Later the building served as City Hall and as the first public school for blacks. Zion Lutheran Church, adjacent to the museum and entered through a lovely garden, is a redbrick German gothic structure built in the 1840s. There is still a German-language Sunday service, and several German-born pastors are buried in the courtyard. Walk your bike through the courtyard to Gay Street.

5.6 *Turn right on Gay Street, walking your bike on the sidewalk.*

5.7 *Turn left on Baltimore Street.*

5.9 *Cross the Fallsway expressway at the light and continue to the*

Baltimore Shot Tower, on your left. Continue on Baltimore Street just past the Shot Tower and take the first right, onto Albemarle Street.

The 215-foot redbrick tower was erected in 1828 for the purpose of manufacturing shot. The method was crude but effective: Molten lead poured through sieves from platforms near the top formed pellets that turned hard when they finally fell into a water "quenching" tank at the bottom.

6.1 *To your right, on the corner of Albemarle and Pratt Streets, stands the Star-Spangled Banner House.*

Here, in 1813, Mary Young Pickersgill sewed the oversized flag that flew over Fort McHenry and inspired Francis Scott Key. Ms. Pickersgill was responding to a request from the fort's commandant, Maj. George Armistead, "to have a flag so large that the British will have no difficulty in seeing it from a distance." The banner, which measured 30 feet by 42 feet and was sewn from 400 yards of wool, now hangs in the Smithsonian Institution in Washington, DC. Continue down Albemarle Street into Little Italy, a treasure-trove of Italian restaurants. The house at 235 Albemarle, to your left, has a painted screen, a rare type of folk art. These hark back to the days before widespread air-conditioning. The scenery painted on the screen provided privacy while letting in fresh air.

6.2 *Turn right on Fawn Street.*

6.3 *Cross South President Street to Columbus Piazza, where a statue of the great explorer gazes out over Baltimore Harbor. Traverse the plaza and cross a bridge. Then ride around a circle and follow signs to a pedestrian bridge.*

Before crossing the pedestrian bridge you may want to stop to look at the Seven Foot Knoll Lighthouse, which originally guarded the entrance to the harbor. Built in 1856, it is Maryland's oldest surviving screwpile lighthouse.

7.0 *After crossing two pedestrian bridges, you will be in the thick of Baltimore's Inner Harbor development.*

You will have to guide your bike through the sea of pedestrians who flock here to visit the aquarium, the maritime museum, the U.S.S. Constellation, or just to eat, shop, and ride the pedal boats.

7.2 *To your left, along the quay, is the water-taxi stop, an alternative means of transportation back to Fort McHenry.*

7.4 *To your right is the Maryland Science Center, an excellent hands-on museum.*

7.6 *Rash Park, to your right, contains a mast memorializing the captain and crew of the Pride of Baltimore, lost at sea in 1986. Walk through the park, carry your bike up the steps to the sidewalk along Key Highway, and turn left.*

7.7 *Cross Key Highway at the light and turn right on Covington Street, which skirts Federal Hill Park.*

From the top of the hill, the view of the city and harbor is spectacular. The hill is so named because a parade to celebrate Maryland's ratification of the Constitution in 1788 ended here.

8.3 *Turn left on Fort Avenue.*

9.6 *Re-enter Fort McHenry.*

9.8 *Arrive back at the parking lot.*

Bicycle Repair Service

Light Street Cycles, 1015 Light Street, Baltimore; 410-685-2234
  Rentals

GREATER WASHINGTON

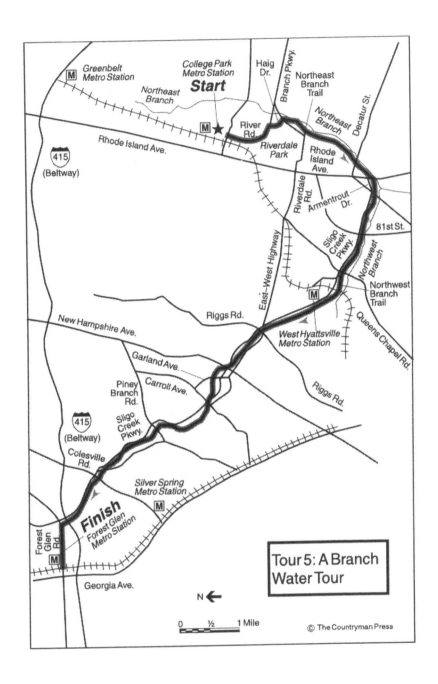

M Greenbelt Metro Station

Northeast Branch

College Park Metro Station **Start**

Haig Dr.

Branch Pkwy.

Northeast Branch Trail

Decatur St.

Northeast Branch

M River Rd ★

Riverdale Park

Rhode Island Ave.

415 (Beltway)

Rhode Island Ave.

Riverdale Rd.

Armentrout Dr.

81st St.

Sligo Creek Pkwy.

Northwest Branch

East-West Highway

Riggs Rd.

M Northwest Branch Trail

West Hyattsville Metro Station

Queens Chapel Rd.

New Hampshire Ave.

Garland Ave.

Carroll Ave.

Riggs Rd.

Piney Branch Rd.

415 (Beltway)

Sligo Creek Pkwy.

Colesville Rd.

Silver Spring Metro Station

M

Finish

Forest Glen Metro Station

Forest Glen Rd.

M

Georgia Ave.

Tour 5: A Branch Water Tour

N ←

0   ½   1 Mile

© The Countryman Press

5
A Branch Water Tour

Location: *Prince George's and Montgomery Counties*
Terrain: *Mainly flat*
Road conditions: *Paved trails with short distances on light-traffic roads*
Distance: *12.9 miles*
Highlights: *The Northeast and Northwest Branches of the Anacostia River, Sligo Creek*

Ever wonder where all that water in the Chesapeake Bay comes from? The Potomac River Basin, a massive network of more than one hundred rivers draining over nearly 15,000 square miles of land provides about one-fifth of the bay's water, and the Anacostia River is an important part of this basin. In Washington, the Anacostia, which comes from a Native American word meaning "town of traders," is a broad estuary and the focus of a recent environmental effort. This tour, however, stays upstream, exploring the narrow, streamlike Northeast and Northwest Branches of the river, and Sligo Creek, a wooded tributary of the Northwest Branch. Fortunately for cyclists, walkers, joggers, birders, in-line skaters, and others, local governments had the foresight to turn the banks of these waterways into parkland, and the Anacostia Tributary Trail System provides miles of uninterrupted trails along these and other branches. The tour begins at the College Park station on Metro's Green Line and quickly joins the Northeast Branch Trail, heading downstream. Where the Northeast and Northwest Branches converge, the tour heads upstream along the Northwest Branch Trail, then branches out onto the Sligo Creek Trail. After following Sligo Creek through woods, parkland, and residential backyards, the tour ends at the Forest Glen station on Metro's Red Line.

0.0 From the east side of the College Park Metro station, turn right onto River Road, which arcs through a wooded industrial park.

0.8 At Haig Drive, just before a bridge, turn right into Riverdale Park. Follow the park road around to your right, past a playground and ball fields, to the Northeast Branch Trail.

1.6 After crossing Riverdale Road, the trail continues through a meadowlike flood plain above the Northeast Branch.

2.6 The trail crosses Decatur Street.

3.1 At the trail intersection, make a sharp right, following the red sign to the Northwest Branch Trail. At the top of the ramp, turn left on Armentrout Drive.

3.4 Cross Rhode Island Avenue at the light and enter Melrose Park, turning right on the Northwest Branch Trail, which traverses a meadow alongside the Northwest Branch.

4.0 Cross 38th Street into 38th Avenue Neighborhood Park.

4.3 Cross the narrow branch on a footbridge.

4.7 The trail recrosses the branch, then crosses Queens Chapel Road and continues through a wooded area and under the Metro tracks.

5.4 Turn right over the smaller of two bridges and cycle through a playground.

5.5 Turn left over another bridge, which leads into the Sligo Creek Trail, which runs along a rise between Sligo Parkway and the soccer fields in Green Meadow Community Park.

6.5 The trail ends. Continue along Sligo Parkway and cross Riggs Road. Pick up the trail again behind the Rite-Aid drug store.

7.0 The trail crosses East-West Highway.

7.9 After crossing a bridge, turn left, go past a basketball court, and follow trail signs across New Hampshire Avenue.

8.3 At the intersection with Garland Avenue, follow the bike route sign to the left.

10.0 Cross Piney Branch Road into a particularly sylvan part of the

The Sligo Creek Trail leads cyclists along a sylvan stream that feeds the Anacostia River.

trail shaded by tall old trees and containing many spots in which to sit and rest along the clear, babbling creek.

11.4 Cross Colesville Road.

12.4 The trail passes under the beltway.

12.5 Turn left on Forest Glen Road, climbing a hill past Holy Cross Hospital.

13.1 Cross Georgia Avenue.

13.3 Turn right into the Forest Glen Metro station.

Bicycle Repair Services

Riverdale Cycle and Fitness, 4503 Queensbury Road, Riverdale; 301-864-4731
No rentals
College Park Bicycles, 4360 Knox Street, College Park; 301-864-2211
Rentals

6
"So We Beat On . . ."

Location: Montgomery County
Terrain: Flat to rolling
Road conditions: Paved, busy roads with shoulders and a paved trail
Distance: 13.2 miles
Highlights: The graves of Scott and Zelda Fitzgerald, the Rock Creek
Hiker-Biker Trail, the romantic architecture of Forest Glen

This tour begins at the Rockville Metro station, a few pedals away from St. Mary's Cemetery, final resting place of Jazz Age legends Scott and Zelda Fitzgerald. The inscription on Francis Scott Key Fitzgerald's tombstone is the last line of his blockbuster novel *The Great Gatsby*: "So we beat on, boats against the current, borne back ceaselessly into the past."

After visiting the graves, the tour beats on, down a short stretch of busy Veirs Mill Road, and then enters the verdant Rock Creek Hiker-Biker Trail, which follows its namesake creek and emerges from the woods at intervals in meadows used as soccer and baseball fields. After a dramatic vista of the Mormon Temple, the tour follows a side trail to Forest Glen Annex of Walter Reed Hospital, a gold mine of eccentric buildings left over from a turn-of-the-twentieth-century finishing school. The tour ends at the Forest Glen Metro station, whence the Metro will bear you effortlessly back to the starting point.

0.0 *Exit the Rockville Metro station onto South Stonestreet Avenue and turn right.*

0.2 *To your right you will see a short flight of steps leading to a pedestrian bridge over the Metro tracks. Carry your bike up the steps and across the bridge. At the end of the bridge, turn right, riding on the sidewalk to the St. Mary's Church complex,*

49

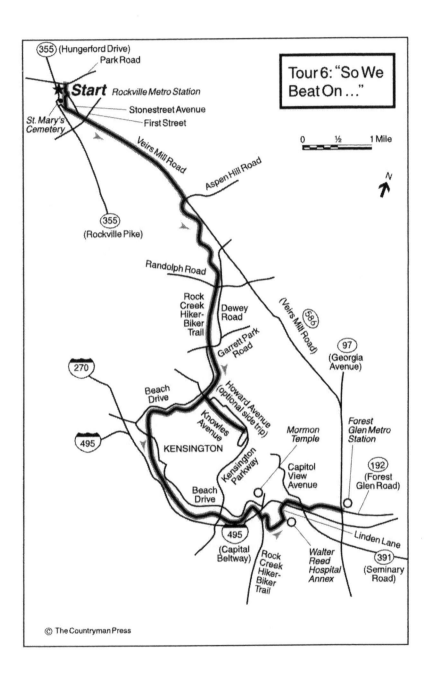

355 (Hungerford Drive)
Park Road

Start Rockville Metro Station

Stonestreet Avenue
First Street

St. Mary's
Cemetery

Veirs Mill Road

Aspen Hill Road

355
(Rockville Pike)

Randolph Road

Rock
Creek
Hiker-
Biker
Trail

Dewey
Road

(Veirs Mill Road)

586

97
(Georgia
Avenue)

Garrett Park
Road

270

Howard Avenue
(optional side trip)

Beach
Drive

Knowles
Avenue

495

KENSINGTON

Mormon
Temple

Forest
Glen Metro
Station

192
(Forest
Glen Road)

Kensington
Parkway

Capitol
View
Avenue

Beach
Drive

495
(Capital
Beltway)

Rock
Creek
Hiker-
Biker
Trail

Walter
Reed
Hospital
Annex

Linden Lane

391
(Seminary
Road)

Tour 6: "So We
Beat On …"

0   ½   1 Mile

N

© The Countryman Press

to your right. Take the driveway past both the modern church and the old church (built in 1817) to the cemetery.

The numerous Fitzgerald graves are found near the back of the cemetery, surrounded by boxwoods and shaded by old oaks.

Although F. Scott Fitzgerald was born in St. Paul, Minnesota, his family had deep roots in Maryland and was related to "Star-Spangled Banner" author Francis Scott Key. When he died in 1940, the poet laureate of the Roaring Twenties was not in good standing with the Roman Catholic Church, which refused to allow him to be buried among his ancestors at St. Mary's. Instead, he was exiled to a nonsectarian burying ground a few miles away. Years later, after the church had mellowed a bit, both Scott and Zelda, who died in a 1948 fire at a mental hospital, were moved to the Fitzgerald plot at St. Mary's. Their daughter, Scotty, joined them in 1986.

Although the cemetery stands at a very busy, three-road inter-section, the tall trees and the adjacent old brick church lend a certain tranquility. One is reminded of a passage in Fitzgerald's *Tender is the Night,* in which Dick Diver attends his father's funeral:

> . . . at the churchyard his father was laid among a hundred Divers, Dorseys, and Hunters. It was very friendly leaving him there with all his rela-tions around him. Flowers were scattered on the brown unsettled earth. Dick had no more ties there now and did not believe he would come back . . .

Fitzgerald, however, did come back, albeit by a circuitous route.

0.4 *After visiting the cemetery, exit the church grounds and turn left, retracing your path past the footbridge and riding on the sidewalk along busy Veirs Mill Road (MD 586), which goes over the Metro tracks on a bridge. At the first traffic light, cross Veirs Mill Road and continue on the sidewalk on the other side.*

When the sidewalk ends, there is a frontage road, and when that ends, there is a shoulder.

3.2 *At the intersection with Aspen Hill Road, turn right onto the Rock Creek Hiker-Biker Trail, which winds through a narrow greenbelt all the way to Washington.*

The trail is paved and well marked. At intervals the woods give way to groomed meadows where you can stop to watch a soccer game in practice—often a skilled and spirited contest between members of one of the area's immigrant communities.

7.0 *At the intersection with Knowles Avenue, you can turn left and go 0.7 mile to the Howard Avenue antique district of Kensington.*

This will add 1.4 miles to your trip.

11.0 *Almost directly in front of you looms the Mormon Temple, an exuberant, soaring white-marble structure topped by a bronze trumpeting angel, Moroni.*

Mormons believe that Moroni lived in America in the fourth century A.D. and compiled the Book of Mormon. It was Moroni who appeared to Joseph Smith in 1827 and instructed him to found the Church of Jesus Christ of Latter-Day Saints. The temple, completed in 1974, has an Oz-like quality that once prompted a prankster to scrawl "Surrender Dorothy" on its fence.

11.5 *At the sign for the Walter Reed Annex and Forest Glen Metro, turn left, following the Bike Route signs and keeping left.*

This will take you onto the grounds of the Walter Reed Army Hospital's Forest Glen Annex.

12.1 *After leaving the bike trail, turn left on Linden Lane.*

Originally a resort, Forest Glen was acquired in 1894 for use as a girls' finishing school, the National Park Seminary. Over the next thirty years or so, a series of eccentric buildings were constructed to house the students. In 1942, the Army took over, and the school closed.

12.3 *At the intersection with Woodstock Avenue, continue on Linden Lane.*

12.4 *The shingled Japanese pagoda on your right, now a private residence, was once a sorority house and later housed Army*

officers. It is now unoccupied, and a group of volunteer history buffs is working to restore it. Follow Linden Lane down the hill, out of the annex grounds, and across the beltway.

12.6 Turn right on Forest Glen Road.

12.9 Turn left into the Forest Glen Metro station.

Bicycle Repair Services

Performance Bike Shop, 1667 Rockville Pike, Rockville; 301-468-0808
   No rentals
Hudson Trail Outfitters, Ltd., 10285 Rockville Pike, Rockville; 301-948-2474
   No rentals

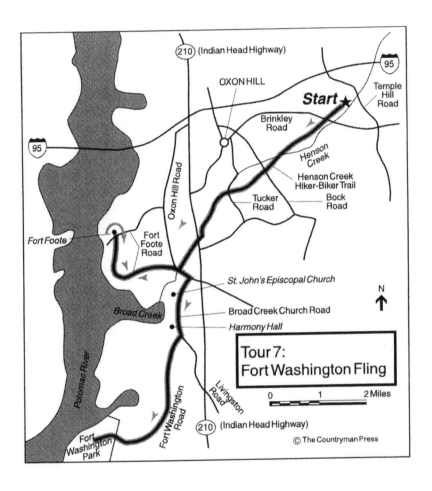

210 (Indian Head Highway)

95

OXON HILL

Start ★

Temple Hill Road

Brinkley Road

Henson Creek

95

Oxon Hill Road

Henson Creek Hiker-Biker Trail

Tucker Road

Bock Road

Fort Foote

Fort Foote Road

St. John's Episcopal Church

Broad Creek

Broad Creek Church Road

Harmony Hall

N

Tour 7:
Fort Washington Fling

Potomac River

0   1   2 Miles

Fort Washington Road

Livingston Road

210 (Indian Head Highway)

© The Countryman Press

Fort Washington Park

7
Fort Washington Fling

Location: *Prince George's County*
Terrain: *Moderately hilly*
Road conditions: *Off-road bike trail, suburban streets, park roads*
Distance: *16.6 miles*
Highlights: *The Henson Creek Trail, Fort Foote, St. John's Episcopal Church, Fort Washington*

The Henson Creek Hiker-Biker Trail runs downstream from Oxon Hill through wooded parkland. The creek flows into Broad Creek and then into the Potomac River, but the trail stops short. The tour follows suburban streets to the remains of Fort Foote, a battlement built to defend the city of Washington during the Civil War. Next stop is the historic St. John's Episcopal Church at Broad Creek, where Washington worshiped. The tour ends at Fort Washington, designed by the cantankerous Pierre L'Enfant, who laid out the federal city.

0.0 *Pick up the trail at the end of Old Temple Hills Road, off Temple Hill Road just north of Brinkley Road.*

The trail travels through woods and meadows, following the stream.

0.8 *Emerging from parkland, the trail continues on the other side of Brinkley Road, a little to the right.*

2.8 *The trail crosses Bock Road and continues through parkland, leading around a small lake.*

There are rest rooms near the tennis courts.

4.0 *At the Tucker Road Ice Rink, cross Tucker Road and pick up the trail again, a little to the left.*

This is the prettiest part of the trail, through woods and marshland and across the stream on arched wooden bridges.

6.0 *The trail passes under Indian Head Highway, reemerges behind some suburban backyards, and leads up a small hill.*

7.0 *The trail ends at Oxon Hill Road. Turn right on Oxon Hill Road and then make an immediate left onto South Fort Foote Road, which winds through a suburban neighborhood.*

8.3 *Look left for views of the Potomac River.*

8.8 *Turn left into Fort Foote Park and follow a dirt path to the ruins of Fort Foote.*

Named for Rear Admiral Andrew Hull Foote, who died of wounds suffered in the Mississippi River campaign, this was one of the most elaborate and best equipped of the 68 forts built to protect the capital from the Confederates. Many dignitaries, including Lincoln himself, visited the earthworks garrison, high on a bluff above the Potomac. On one occasion, Lincoln and his party traveled down the river on a paddle-wheeler and were entertained at the fort by its commandant, who was Secretary Seward's son. The dignitaries ate local peaches and drank champagne. The fort's heavy guns, which weighed 49,000 pounds, could fire 500-pound cannon balls 3 miles down the river. The fort's prowess was never tested, for no hostile forces sailed up the Potomac. Its only casualties were due to malaria. The fort was abandoned in 1878 and left to ruin. During the 1980s, it was partially restored, with some of the 15-inch Rodman guns remounted.

9.1 *After visiting the fort, exit the park and backtrack on Fort Foote Road.*

10.8 *Turn right on Oxon Hill Road, watching for traffic as you descend a hill.*

11.2 *Turn right on Broad Creek Church Road to St. John's Episcopal Church, which dates from 1766.*

Credible evidence and honest tradition record that Washington attended services here on numerous occasions, reads the historical marker. Mount Vernon lies a short cruise across the Potomac, and a trip to St. John's would have been easier than an overland coach

Built in 1824 on the Potomac River to guard the nation's capital, Fort
Washington is now a national park.

trip. In the churchyard are graves of three Revolutionary War
soldiers.

11.5 *Exit the church grounds on Old St. John's Way.*

11.6 *Turn right on Livingston Road. Watch for traffic.*

12.4 *On your right is Harmony Hall, currently under restoration.*
The two-and-a-half-story Georgian brick house, built about 1750,
was originally named Battersea. The name was changed after the
locally prominent Addison brothers brought their brides here in
1792. The two couples lived here in such harmony that the house
was rechristened.

12.9 *Turn right on Fort Washington Road.*

15.8 *At the top of the hill, look to the right for a view of the river
with the Washington Monument in the distance.*

16.4 *Enter Fort Washington Park, a National Park Service property.*

16.6 *Arrive at the visitors center and the fort.*

Built in 1808 as Fort Warburton, the fort was built to protect the capital from the British if tensions between the two nations grew into a full-fledged war, which they did. On August 20, 1814, British warships sailed up the Potomac. Fort Warburton's commandant, Capt. Samuel Dyson, evacuated his men and blew up the fort so it wouldn't fall into British hands. Reconstruction began almost immediately, under the direction of the temperamental Pierre L'Enfant, the architect who planned the capital city. L'Enfant's inability to get along with the powers that held the purse strings—plus diminishing interest in defense after the Treaty of Ghent—strung out the project, which was finally completed, though not yet armed, in 1824. Twenty-some years later, with sectional tensions rising, the fortifications were strengthened and cannons were installed to defend the capital against a waterborne Confederate attack, which never occurred. Today, visitors can walk across the drawbridge and under the magnificent stone arch into the parade grounds, lined by barracks and officers' quarters. From the ramparts, there are wonderful views in all directions. The park also has a lighthouse, picnic areas, miles of trails, and sports facilities.

Bicycle Repair Service

Riverdale Cycle and Fitness, 4503 Queensbury Road, Riverdale; 301-864 4731
No rentals

8
Inter-Suburb Sprint

Location: *Montgomery County*
Terrain: *Mostly flat with a few moderate hills*
Road conditions: *Dirt-and-gravel trail and some roads with light traffic*
Distance: *6.2 miles*
Highlights: *The trestle over Rock Creek, ethnic restaurants of Silver Spring*

From 1889 until 1985, the Georgetown Branch rail line of the Baltimore & Ohio Railroad hauled coal and building materials from Georgetown, in the District of Columbia, to the once-outpost and now-urban areas of Chevy Chase, Bethesda, and Silver Spring, all in Maryland. The decreasing need for coal, the transformation of the Georgetown waterfront from an industrial port to a tourist attraction, and the decline of railroads generally combined to bring about the line's demise. The year after the line was abandoned, a group of citizens formed The Capital Crescent Trail Coalition with the goal of turning the unused rail bed into a multiuse trail. The group succeeded in having the National Park Service purchase and develop the section from Georgetown to Bethesda and persuaded Montgomery County to buy the section from Bethesda to Silver Spring.

The Capital Crescent Trail is paved from Georgetown to Bethesda. The remainder of the trail, from Bethesda to Silver Spring, is a packed gravel work-in-progress, known as the "Interim Trail," the "Georgetown Branch Trail," or the "Future Capital Crescent Trail."

This tour explores the Georgetown Branch Trail from the Bethesda Metro station to the trail terminus in Silver Spring and then makes its way to the Silver Spring Metro station.

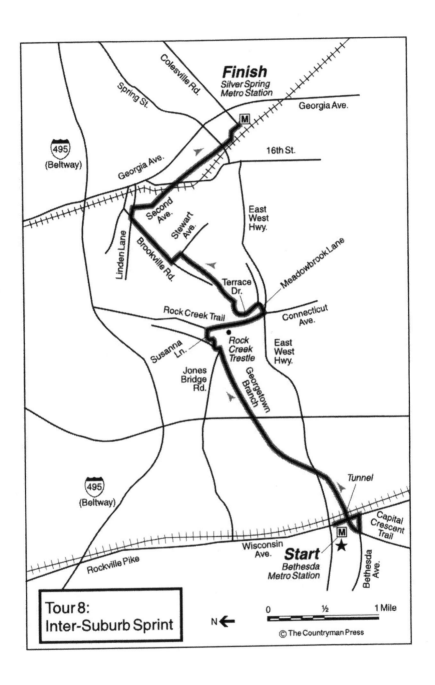

Finish
Silver Spring
Metro Station

Colesville Rd.

Spring St.

Georgia Ave.

Ⓜ

Georgia Ave.

16th St.

495
(Beltway)

Second
Ave.

Stewart
Ave.

East
West
Hwy.

Linden Lane

Brookville Rd.

Terrace
Dr.

Meadowbrook Lane

Rock Creek Trail

Connecticut
Ave.

Susanna
Ln.

Rock
Creek
Trestle

East
West
Hwy.

Jones
Bridge
Rd.

Georgetown
Branch

495
(Beltway)

Tunnel

Capital
Crescent
Trail

Ⓜ

Wisconsin
Ave.

Start
Bethesda
Metro Station

★

Bethesda
Ave.

Rockville Pike

Tour 8:
Inter-Suburb Sprint

N ←

0   ½   1 Mile

© The Countryman Press

0.0 *From the elevator of the Bethesda Metro station, on the Red line, turn right on Wisconsin Avenue.*

0.2 *Turn right on Bethesda Avenue.*

0.3 *Turn right into the tunnel that leads under Wisconsin Avenue.*

0.6 *Reemerging from the tunnel, the trail travels through pleasant, wooded backyards and traverses the Columbia Country Club.*

1.7 *Cross Connecticut Avenue at the light, bear left, and rejoin the trail.*

2.5 *The trail ends—temporarily—at Jones Bridge Road. This detour is necessary because the old railroad trestle that will eventually take the trail over Rock Creek has not yet been rebuilt. In the interim, turn left on the sidewalk, cross Jones Bridge Road, and turn right into Susanna Lane, which leads into Rock Creek Park.*

2.8 *Turn right at the green sign, following both the Rock Creek Hiker-Biker Trail and the Georgetown Branch Trail.*

3.1 *Pass under the Rock Creek trestle, the future route of the completed Capitol Crescent Trail.*

The trestle, built in the 1890s, was initially 1,400 feet long and 67 feet high, the largest of its type in the B&O system. In 1904, the span was reduced to 281 feet by filling in some of the gap between the two sides. The trestle was rebuilt in 1928 and again in 1972, after Hurricane Agnes.

3.3 *In the park—athletic field known as Ray's Meadow, turn left, following the sign, up the stairs and through the parking lot. Then turn left on Meadowbrook Lane, which climbs a hill.*

3.6 *Turn left on Terrace Drive and continue straight into the trail, which travels through a semi-industrial area.*

4.2 *The trail ends on Stewart Avenue. Turn left, continue half a block up a slight hill, and turn right on Brookville Road.*

4.9 *Turn right on Linden Lane.*

5.0 *Turn right on Second Avenue.*

The Georgetown Branch Trail—an extension of the popular Capital Crescent Trail—joins the Rock Creek Trail, then diverges from it and leads into Silver Spring.

6.2 *Turn right into the Silver Spring Metro station. Or continue to Georgia Avenue, which has several ethnic restaurants.*

Bicycle Repair Service

Big Wheel Bikes, 6917 Arlington Road, Bethesda; 301-652-0192
No rentals

ANNAPOLIS AREA

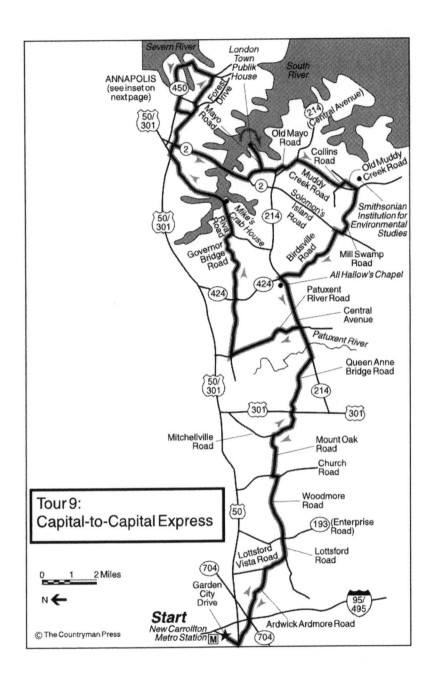

9
Capital-to-Capital Express

Location: *Prince George's and Anne Arundel Counties*
Terrain: *Moderately hilly*
Road conditions: *Paved roads, a few with heavy traffic*
Distance: *64.5 miles*
Highlights: *Historic Annapolis, the U.S. Naval Academy, Maryland's capitol, St. John's College, London Town Publik House and Gardens*

Annapolis has been a capital for a much longer time than has Washington—since 1694. And it is one of several cities that served as temporary capital of the new United States. The Continental Congress ratified the Treaty of Paris here, officially ending the Revolution. Since then, Annapolis has been invaded by armies of legislators, Naval Academy Middies and their more counterculture counterparts at St. John's College, boaters, and yachting wannabes, but it has retained the flavor of a colonial port city and kept most of its original architecture intact.

In fair weather, the highway to Annapolis from Washington is paved with blocked traffic. Fortunately, you can get there by bicycle—on much more pleasant roads.

The tour begins at the New Carrollton Metro station, which you can get to by Metro (see the Introduction, "About Metrorail"), or where you can park your car free on weekends.

0.0 Exit the New Carrollton Metro station on the east side, following the bus lane. Turn right onto Garden City Drive, then left at the V, under US 50. Continue to the left on Ardwick Ardmore Road.

3.4 Ardwick Ardmore Road ends in front of the Enterprise Golf Club. Turn right on Lottsford Vista Road. This will take you down a hill and along a pleasant stream.

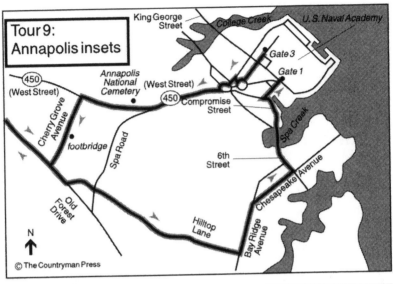

Tour 9:
Annapolis insets

King George Street

College Creek

U. S. Naval Academy

Gate 3

Gate 1

450
(West Street)

Annapolis National Cemetery

(West Street)

450

Compromise Street

Cherry Grove Avenue

footbridge

Spa Road

6th Street

Spa Creek

Chesapeake Avenue

Old Forest Drive

Hilltop Lane

Bay Ridge Avenue

N

© The Countryman Press

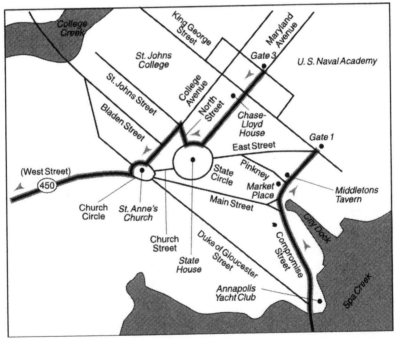

College Creek

King George Street

Maryland Avenue

St. Johns College

Gate 3

U. S. Naval Academy

St. Johns Street

College Avenue

North Street

Bladen Street

Chase-Lloyd House

Gate 1

East Street

(West Street)

450

State Circle

Pinkney

Church Circle

St. Anne's Church

Main Street

Market Place

Middletons Tavern

Church Street

Duke of Gloucester Street

Compromise Street

City Dock

State House

Annapolis Yacht Club

Spa Creek

4.2 *Lottsford Vista Road ends. Turn left on Lottsford Road, which climbs a mild hill.*

4.8 *Lottsford Road ends at Enterprise Road (MD 193). Cross Enterprise Road at the light and continue straight on Woodmore Road.*

5.3 *The white clapboard Holy Family Church, set amid tall trees, dates from 1890.*

7.3 *At Mount Oak Cemetery, turn left on Church Road.*

7.4 *At Mount Oak Methodist Church, built in 1881, turn right on Mount Oak Road, a rolling, country road.*

8.9 *Turn right on Mitchellville Road, after stopping at the convenience store at the intersection for refreshment.*

This is a busy road, but there are little-used sidewalks.

10.3 *Cross both lanes of US 301—very carefully. On the other side of the highway, Mitchellville Road turns into Queen Anne Bridge Road, which winds up a hill and through a rural area.*

12.5 *Turn left on Central Avenue (MD 214). Watch for traffic as you follow this busy road across the Patuxent River on a bridge.*

13.7 *Turn left on Patuxent River Road, which follows the river.*

The road, and the river, are lined with sand and gravel operations. On weekends, however, the road is quiet and pleasant.

17.0 *Turn right on Governor Bridge Road.*

21.8 *Turn left on Riva Road.*

Since Annapolis is located on a neck, accessible only by a few roads, there are no low-traffic roads to get there from here. Use caution.

23.3 *After Mike's Crab House, to your right, watch for storm grates on the bridge.*

Mike's is a good place to refresh yourself and sample local specialties. It sits on the banks of the South River and affords great views from the deck and dock.

26.0 *Turn right on Forest Drive.*

27.8 *Bear left on Hilltop Lane and follow it through a residential area.*

29.1 *Turn left on Bay Ridge Avenue.*

29.5 *At the V, bear right on Chesapeake Avenue.*

29.8 *Turn left on Sixth Street, which leads to a bridge across Spa Creek and becomes Compromise Street.*

> You may not be able to see the waters of Spa Creek because of the proverbial forest of masts. On your right, as soon as you cross the bridge, is the Annapolis Yacht Club.

30.1 *Just past the Annapolis Summer Garden Theater, to your left, at a small circle, turn right on Randall Street.*

> On your right is the City Dock, where fisherfolk have been almost totally supplanted by the Top-Sider set. On your left is a 1970 replacement of the Market House that had stood in this space since 1728. The current building holds food stands. Just beyond the Market House is the Middleton Tavern, whose all-header bond facade testifies to its early-eighteenth-century origin. It once served as a custom house and is now serving its original function as a watering place and restaurant.

30.3 *Turn left in front of the Middleton, then make a sharp left onto Pinckney Street. Retrace your way to Randall Street, which leads to the U.S. Naval Academy gate.*

> At 18 Pinckney Street stands the Slicer-Shiplap House, which dates from 1723 and was built with ship planking.

30.5 *Enter the academy grounds (bike helmets required).*

> At a visitors center to your right you may sign up for a guided tour, or you may ride around on your own. Of special note is the domed chapel, whose stained-glass windows honor naval heroes, and a crypt containing the sarcophagus of John Paul Jones. The father of the American Navy died in Paris in 1792, after a stint in Russia where he was reportedly the lover of Catherine the Great. His remains were moved to Annapolis in 1905.

31.5 *Exit the academy through Gate 3 onto Maryland Avenue, a narrow cobblestoned street.*

A cobblestone street leads to Maryland's State House.

On your right, after crossing King George Street, you will see the Chase-Lloyd House, a Georgian mansion from Annapolis's "golden age," the late eighteenth century.

31.7 *Climbing a slight hill, Maryland Avenue runs into State Circle.*

State Circle is the site of the State House, completed just after the Revolution. It is open for tours daily.

31.9 *At about 2 o'clock on State Circle, turn right on North Street and follow it 1 block.*

32.0 *Cross College Avenue and enter the campus of St. John's College.*

St. John's dates from colonial times and bases its curriculum on the reading of great books. Unfortunately, St. John's venerable Liberty Tree, a tulip poplar that shaded Revolutionary conspirators against the British, was mortally wounded by Hurricane Floyd in 1999. The remainder of the tree was cut down in a funeral-like ceremony, and University of Maryland biotechnology researchers are trying to clone the tree from material taken from the original.

After leaving the campus, turn left on College Avenue and follow it to Church Circle, named for St. Anne's Church, to your right, completed in 1792.

32.2 *At 12 o'clock on the circle, turn right on West Street (MD 450). Watch for traffic.*

33.0 *On your right is Annapolis National Cemetery, final resting place of many unknown Civil War soldiers.*

33.5 *Turn left on Cherry Grove Avenue, which is not a through street for cars. Cyclists may take advantage of a footbridge, however.*

34.1 *Turn right on Forest Drive.*

35.4 *Turn left on Solomons Island Road (MD 2). Ride on the shoulder.*

38.2 *Cross the South River on a bridge.*

39.3 *Turn left on Mayo Road.*

40.1 *Turn left on London Town Road.*

41.3 At the end of the road, turn left into the London Town Publik House and Gardens.

The attraction is open Tuesday through Sunday except in January and February. There is an admission fee.

An early-eighteenth-century boomtown, London Town was the site of a ferry across the South River to Annapolis. The Publik House was built circa 1760 by ferry operator William Brown to house and feed waiting passengers. Docents give excellent tours, and the surrounding gardens are spectacular. After touring the house and gardens, double back on London Town Road.

43.1 Turn left on Mayo Road.

43.5 Bear left on Old Mayo Road.

43.9 Turn left on Central Avenue (MD 214).

44.3 Turn right on Muddy Creek Road.

46.2 Turn left on Collins Road.

46.5 Turn right on Old Muddy Creek Road, which skirts the Smithsonian Institution for Environmental Studies.

This facility has programs for schools and other groups.

46.6 Old Muddy Creek Road crosses Muddy Creek Road and becomes Mill Swamp Road, which climbs a hill.

48.4 Turn right on Solomons Island Road (MD 2). Watch for traffic.

48.6 Turn left on Birdsville Road.

51.6 Turn left on Central Avenue (MD 214). A market and deli are at the intersection.

51.8 All Hallows Chapel, on your right, has an inviting graveyard in which to eat the food purchased at the market.

54.3 Cross the Patuxent River on a bridge.

54.8 Turn right on Queen Anne Bridge Road.

56.0 After crossing US 301, Queen Anne Bridge Road becomes Mitchellville Road.

57.4 Turn left on Mount Oak Road.

58.9 Turn left on Church Road.

59.0 Turn right on Woodmore Road.

59.4 Cross Enterprise Road and continue straight on Lottsford Road.

60.0 Turn right on Lottsford Vista Road.

60.9 Turn left on Ardwick-Ardmore Road.

63.9 Turn right on Pennsy Drive and go over a bridge.

64.2 Turn left on Corporate Drive.

64.5 Enter Metro station.

Bicycle Repair Services

South River Cycle, 117A Mayo Road, Edgewater; 410-956-6310
    No rentals
George's Bicycle Repair, 1556 Patuxent Manor Court, Davidsonville;
    410-798-5607
    No rentals

Accommodations

Historic Inns of Annapolis: 1-800-638-8902 in Maryland, 1-800-847-8882 outside Maryland

10
Quiet Waters Loop

Location: *Anne Arundel County*
Terrain: *Flat to rolling*
Road conditions: *Paved bike path and park road*
Distance: *5.2 miles*
Highlights: *The visitors center art gallery, Harness Creek Overlook, South River Overlook, woodlands*

Jewel-like Quiet Waters Park provides a 336-acre haven for waterfowl, eagles, pileated woodpeckers, great horned owls, bluebirds, foxes, and deer—and a tranquil loop perfect for a short bicycle-trip-cum-picnic. Once a farm, this tract was scheduled in 1986 to be bulldozed for 250 new homes. But neighbors objected and persuaded the county to purchase the land and turn it into a very elegant park, with gazebos, picnic pavilions, a skating rink, footpaths, and a bike trail.

The park is located off Forest Drive on Hillsmere Drive in Annapolis. It is open from dawn to dusk, except Tuesday, and admission is charged for cars. The tour begins at the first parking lot after the entrance, adjacent to the Red Maple Pavilion.

- *0.0 From the parking lot, go past the Sassafras Pavilion and enter the bike path, which winds through thick woods, curving gently.*
- *0.8 Follow the bike path, which curves left. Bikes are not allowed on the footpath, which goes straight ahead.*
- *1.0 At the Dogwood Pavilion, turn left again.*
- *1.1 The Blue Heron Center, to your left, just past the parking lot, is used for weddings and parties.*
- *1.2 The visitors center on your left has a gallery with frequently-*

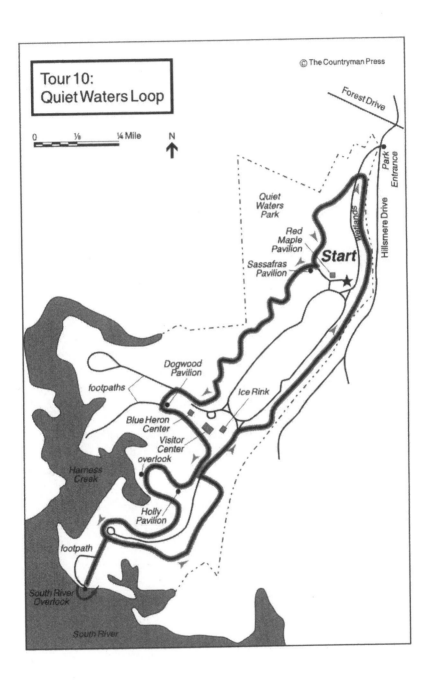

© The Countryman Press

Tour 10:
Quiet Waters Loop

0   ⅛   ¼ Mile

N

Forest Drive

Quiet
Waters
Park

Red
Maple
Pavilion

Sassafras
Pavilion

Start

Wetlands

Park
Entrance

Hillsmere Drive

Dogwood
Pavilion

footpaths

Ice Rink

Blue Heron
Center

Visitor
Center

overlook

Harness
Creek

Holly
Pavilion

footpath

South River
Overlook

South River

changing shows by local artists, as well as rest rooms and a
snack bar.

1.3 *Just past the visitors center, the bike path curves to the right,
going down and then up a hill.*

1.5 *By the Holly Pavilion, the path curves right, back into the
woods.*

1.7 *Stop at the overlook high above quiet Harness Creek, a
favorite anchorage for sailboats. After the overlook, the path
curves left, then right again.*

2.3 *Turn right, following the sign to the South River Overlook.*

2.6 *Park your bike in the rack near the gazebo and drink in a
spectacular view of the mouth of the South River and the
seemingly endless Chesapeake Bay. Steps or a footpath take
you down, level with the river. After your visit, reverse direction
on the bike path.*

2.9 *Turn right on the bike path, which goes through a meadow on
the edge of the woods and curves back to the main park
road.*

3.5 *Turn right on the park road and follow it up the hill to the ice
rink.*

3.7 *Just past the ice rink, on your left, turn right onto the bike
path, which goes through a narrow strip of park with a fence
on one side and a fitness course on the other.*

4.6 *The path skirts some wetlands, then crosses the park road.*

4.9 *After crossing the road, the path reenters the woods.*

5.1 *Just past the maintenance compound to your left, take the
exit to Sassafras Pavilion.*

5.2 *Return to the parking lot.*

Bicycle Repair Service

Bike Doctor, 150 Jennifer Street, Annapolis; 410-266-7383
   No rentals

GREATER FREDERICK AREA

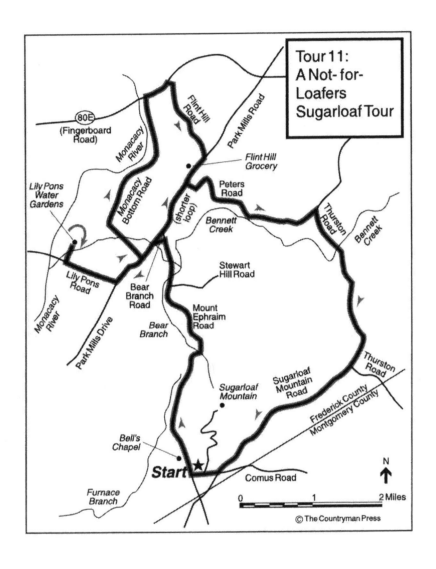

Tour 11:
A Not-for-
Loafers
Sugarloaf Tour

80E
(Fingerboard
Road)

Flint Hill
Road

Park Mills Road

Monacacy River

Flint Hill
Grocery

Lily Pons
Water
Gardens

Monacacy
Bottom Road

Peters
Road

Thurston
Road

Bennett
Creek

(shorter
loop)

Bennett
Creek

Lily Pons
Road

Stewart
Hill Road

Monacacy
River

Bear
Branch
Road

Mount
Ephraim
Road

Park Mills Drive

Bear
Branch

Thurston
Road

Sugarloaf
Mountain

Sugarloaf
Mountain
Road

Frederick County
Montgomery County

Bell's
Chapel

Start ★

N

Comus Road

Furnace
Branch

0   1   2 Miles

© The Countryman Press

11
A Not-for-Loafers Sugarloaf Tour

Location: Frederick County, near the Montgomery County line
Terrain: Hilly
Road conditions: Some dirt-and-gravel roads, light traffic
Distance: 19.2 miles, with a 15.9-mile alternate route
Highlights: Sugarloaf Mountain Park, Lily Pons Water Gardens, the
  Monacacy River

One day in 1902 a wealthy young man named Gordon Strong bicycled from Washington, DC, toward Frederick, Maryland. On his way he caught a glimpse of Sugarloaf Mountain, and it was love at first sight. Strong eventually bought the mountain and built a home, Stronghold, on its slopes. Stronghold now rents out for weddings, and the mountain is the centerpiece of a 3,000-acre park run by the Stronghold Foundation and open to the public since 1926. One visitor, President Franklin Delano Roosevelt, coveted the place and tried to get Strong to sell it to the government for a summer White House. Strong declined but graciously told FDR about the site in the nearby Catoctin Mountains that later became Shangri-La and, still later, Camp David.

Sugarloaf rises dramatically from the rather flat Monacacy Valley to 1,280 feet. The tallest thing around, it was used as a watchtower and signal station by Union troops monitoring Lee's progress toward Antietam.

This tour does not require you to bike all the way from Washington or even to climb the mountain, although older folks and toddlers walk up to the summit on the stone steps regularly. If you do want to climb it, bike or drive to the second parking lot on the mountain before you start the bike tour. It's an easy climb from that point, but after this rigorous ride around the base of Sugarloaf you'll probably be too tired to attempt the climb. The tour begins in the parking lot at the base of the mountain.

81

A cyclist explores an abandoned log cabin on a country road near Sugarloaf Mountain.

0.0 *From the parking lot, follow the road that hugs the base of the mountain, Comus Road, heading west.*

0.5 *Turn right on Mount Ephraim Road, which is hard-packed dirt and gravel.*

0.9 *An old yellow schoolhouse and white-clapboarded Bell's Chapel form a small settlement to your left. Then the road reenters the wooded park, traveling up and down small hills through woods filled with mountain laurel.*

Watch for deer heading down toward Furnace Branch or Bear Branch to drink.

2.5 *Mount Ephraim Road veers to the left, crossing Bear Branch.*

After a rainstorm, there may be water on the road. Equestrian trails crisscross the road in this area, so watch for horses.

3.8 *Just after you pass the intersection with Stewart Hill Road, Mount Ephraim Road becomes paved and crosses Bennett Creek on a concrete bridge.*

4.2 *At the intersection of Bear Branch Road stands a small settlement marked by an abandoned nineteenth-century grocery store, a few houses, and several formidable-looking but friendly dogs. Turn left and follow Bear Branch Road down a hill.*

4.3 *Turn left on Park Mills Road. Watch for traffic. (There is not much, but more than on the roads previously traveled.)*

5.7 *Turn right on Lily Pons Road.*

6.5 *Turn right into Lily Pons Water Gardens.*

This 360-acre aqua-farm has more than four hundred ponds where crops of goldfish and water lilies are raised. The enterprise was originally known as Three Springs Fishery, but when its mail-order business became substantial, in the 1930s, the government agreed to give it its own post office. A punning opera buff suggested naming it after the then-reigning diva of the Metropolitan Opera, and Miss Pons graciously agreed. Visitors are free to wander around the ponds, but there are better views of the fish in the tanks in back of the store. Rest rooms and a soda machine are available.

6.6 *Exit the fish farm and go back to the intersection of Lily Pons Road and Park Mills Road.*

7.4 *Turn left on Park Mills Road.*

7.8 *Turn left on Monacacy Bottom Road, which is unmarked. A white house stands on the corner. (If the weather has been very rainy, or if you really can't stand gravel roads, continue on Park Mills Road to the intersection with Peters Road, a distance of 1.5 miles. Pick up the main tour at the 12.6-mile point.)*

Go slowly on Monacacy Bottom Road, which is gravel. You may want to picnic by the ponds that are part of Lily Pons Water Gardens.

8.6 *The road comes to a branch of the Monacacy River.*

This popular fishing spot is surrounded by woods filled with bluebonnets. In wet seasons, the road is underwater—but, usually, not much water. It's possible and quite pleasant to walk your bike across. People with pick-up trucks may also come to your rescue. Once across, follow Monacacy Bottom Road to the right, up a hill, and through a rural residential neighborhood. Once over the crest, you can coast downhill for a stretch along the broad, flat main branch of the Monacacy, which means "stream of big bends." Native Americans used the Monacacy as part of a canoe trail from New York State to North Carolina.

10.5 *Turn right on Fingerboard Road (MD 80E).*

10.9 *Turn right on Flint Hill Road, which winds up a hill, then along a creek lined with mayapples.*

12.1 *Turn right on Park Mills Road, along a ridge with good views.*

12.4 *Flint Hill Grocery, the only store on the route, is on your right.*

12.6 *At the bottom of a hill, turn left on Peters Road. This is a narrow, hard-packed dirt-and-gravel road through a rural, wooded area with a sheep farm. Once it crests a hill, the road follows Bennett Creek.*

15.0 *Turn right on Thurston Road, which is busier and paved.*

17.3 *Turn right on Sugarloaf Mountain Road, which climbs a hill through woods and farmland.*

18.2 Sugarloaf Mountain Road becomes a dirt-and-gravel road.

19.0 Sugarloaf Mountain Road ends at Comus Road. Turn right on Comus Road.

19.2 Return to the parking lot.

Bicycle Repair Service

Frederick Bicycle Sales and Service, 1216 West Patrick Street, Frederick; 301-663-4452
  No rentals
Bob's Bicycle Service, 19961 Fisher Avenue, Poolesville; 301-605-0211 or 301-253-8761
  Mobile repairs within Montgomery County

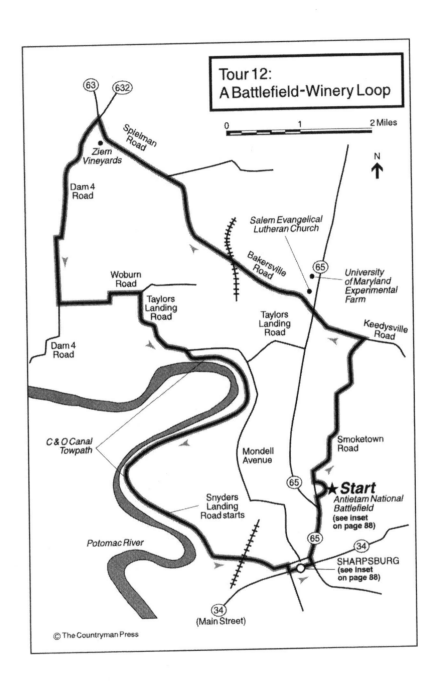

Tour 12:
A Battlefield-Winery Loop

0   1   2 Miles

N

63   632

Spielman Road

Ziem Vineyards

Dam 4 Road

Salem Evangelical Lutheran Church

65

University of Maryland Experimental Farm

Woburn Road

Bakersville Road

Taylors Landing Road

Taylors Landing Road

Keedysville Road

Dam 4 Road

C & O Canal Towpath

Smoketown Road

Mondell Avenue

65

★ Start
Antietam National Battlefield
(see inset on page 88)

Snyders Landing Road starts

65

34

Potomac River

SHARPSBURG
(see inset on page 88)

34
(Main Street)

© The Countryman Press

12
A Battlefield-Winery Loop

Location: *Washington County*
Terrain: *Rolling; flat on the Chesapeake & Ohio Canal towpath*
Road conditions: *Paved country roads and one stretch of dirt road with light traffic; unpaved towpath with some rough spots*
Distance: *21.2 miles*
Highlights: *Antietam National Battlefield, the Ziem Vineyards, the Chesapeake & Ohio Canal*

On September 17, 1862, Union and Confederate troops clashed near Sharpsburg, Maryland. By late afternoon more than twenty-three thousand of them were dead—making that day the bloodiest of the Civil War.

This tour begins at the visitors center of Antietam National Battlefield, where an excellent film interprets the historic battle. It travels through part of the battlefield, then exits the park and continues on country roads to the Ziem Vineyards for a tasting tour of Maryland's westernmost winery. More country roads lead to the Chesapeake & Ohio Canal towpath, between the mostly dried-up canal and the Potomac River. Leaving the towpath, the tour travels through farmland to the nineteenth-century town of Sharpsburg, then returns to the visitors center.

The Antietam National Battlefield Visitor Center is on MD 65 just north of the intersection with MD 34. Admission to the battlefield is free, but there is an admission charge to the visitors center.

0.0 Exit the visitors center parking lot and turn right.

> Just across the road is the Dunker Church, focal point of repeated clashes during the battle. Destroyed by a storm in 1921, it was rebuilt in the original style in 1962.

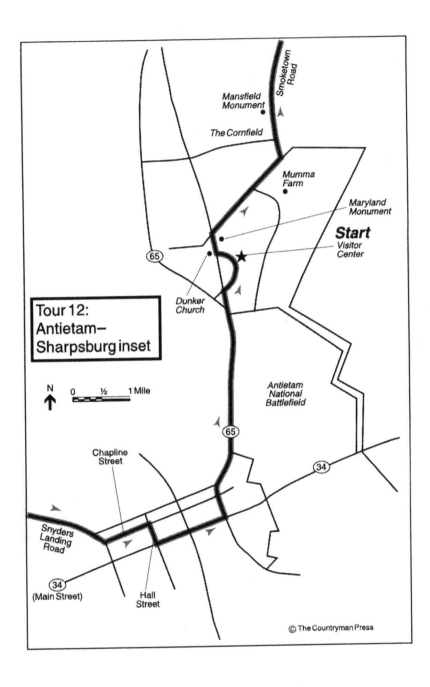

Smoketown Road

Mansfield
Monument

The Cornfield

Mumma
Farm

Maryland
Monument

Start
Visitor
Center

65

Dunker
Church

Tour 12:
Antietam–
Sharpsburg inset

N

0   ½   1 Mile

Antietam
National
Battlefield

Chapline
Street

65

34

Snyders
Landing
Road

34
(Main Street)

Hall
Street

© The Countryman Press

0.1 *In front of the Maryland Monument, erected in memory of Marylanders who died here, bear right on Smoketown Road.*

On your left, in the cornfield of the Miller farm, more fighting took place than anywhere else on the battlefield. According to Union general Joseph Hooker, "every stalk of corn in the northern and greater part of the field was cut as closely as could have been done with a knife, and the slain lay in rows precisely as they had stood in their ranks a few moments before." At the right is the Mumma farm, whose now-restored buildings were burned by Confederates to prevent their use by Union troops.

0.8 *At the left stands a monument to Union general Joseph Mansfield.*

Beyond the Mansfield Monument, Smoketown Road turns into a hard-packed dirt road.

2.4 *Turn left on Keedysville Road.*

At the right is the University of Maryland Experimental Farm.

3.2 *After crossing MD 65, Keedysville Road becomes Bakersville Road and passes Salem Evangelical Lutheran Church, to your right, built in 1854.*

4.6 *After passing under a railroad bridge, Bakersville Road becomes a series of roller-coaster hills.*

6.3 *At the V, bear left on Spielman Road.*

7.4 *Turn left into Ziem Vineyards.*

Winemaker Robert Ziem, a former NASA chemist, personally conducts some tours of the winery, which is housed in a two-hundred-year-old barn. In the tasting room, Ziem's five reds and four whites are offered for sampling and purchase. All are made from the grapes grown at the vineyards.

7.8 *Exiting the vineyard grounds, turn left and continue on Spielman Road.*

8.0 *Bear left at the V and then turn left on Dam No. 4 Road.*

10.8 *Turn left on Woburn Road, which leads past some suburban-type houses and up a modest hill.*

12.1 *Turn right on Taylor's Landing Road for a delightful downhill*

A cyclist pedals past the monument to Union General Joseph K. Mansfield, killed at the Battle of Antietam.

swoop to the Potomac River and the Chesapeake & Ohio Canal towpath.

13.4 Enter the towpath and turn left.

In spring, look for bluebonnets, mayapples, lilies-of-the-valley, and violets along the path. In all seasons you may need to walk your bike around boulders and other rough spots. The canal, and the towpath, follow the river in a wide horseshoe bend. There are some good places for a swim in the Potomac in this stretch.

18.0 Cross the canal on a footbridge and follow Snyders Landing Road, which winds uphill, through verdant woods into a farming area.

18.9 Snyders Landing Road passes under a railroad bridge.

19.4 Turn left on Chapline Street.

19.6 Turn right on Hall Street.

19.8 Turn left on Main Street.

The Jacob Rohrbach house, on the southeast corner of Hall and Main, is now a bed-and-breakfast. Its name reflects the fact that many of the original settlers of this area were German. A Union sympathizer like most of his fellow townspeople, Jacob Rohrbach was killed defending his home from Confederate troops. Like the Rohrbach home, most of the brick houses in this nineteenth-century town are built close to the road.

20.2 Turn left on MD 65.

21.2 Turn right into the visitors center.

Bicycle Repair Services

Hub City Cycle Center, 35 North Prospect, Hagerstown; 301-797-9877
No rentals

Potomac Pushbikes, 11 East Potomac Street, Williamsport; 301-582-4747
Rentals

Reels & Wheels, 17328 Taylors Landing Road, Sharpsburg; 301-432-7281
March to October only

Accommodations

Jacob Rohrbach Inn, 138 West Main Street, Sharpsburg, MD 21782; 301-432-5079

Inn at Antietam, 220 East Main Street, Sharpsburg, MD 21782; 301-432-6601

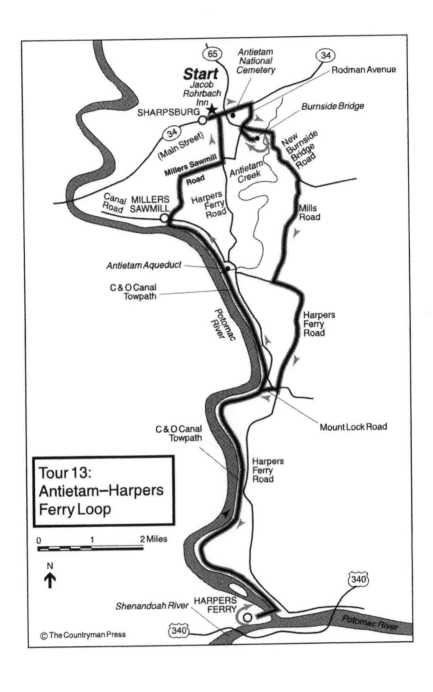

65

Antietam
National
Cemetery

34

Rodman Avenue

Start
*Jacob
Rohrbach
Inn*

SHARPSBURG

Burnside Bridge

34

(Main Street)

New
Burnside
Bridge
Road

Millers Sawmill
Road

Antietam
Creek

Canal
Road

MILLERS
SAWMILL

Harpers
Ferry
Road

Mills
Road

Antietam Aqueduct

C & O Canal
Towpath

Potomac
River

Harpers
Ferry
Road

Mount Lock Road

C & O Canal
Towpath

Harpers
Ferry
Road

Tour 13:
Antietam–Harpers
Ferry Loop

0   1   2 Miles

N

340

Shenandoah River

HARPERS
FERRY

340

Potomac River

© The Countryman Press

13
Antietam–Harpers Ferry Loop

Location: *Washington County*
Terrain: *Moderately hilly; flat on towpath*
Road conditions: *Country roads with light traffic; Chesapeake & Ohio Canal towpath, which is unpaved but easily cycled*
Distance: *27.2 miles*
Highlights: *Antietam National Cemetery; Antietam National Battlefield; the Burnside Bridge; the Chesapeake & Ohio Canal; Harpers Ferry, West Virginia*

In a sense, the Civil War began not at Fort Sumter but at Harpers Ferry, where John Brown fired the shots heard 'round the world. And, although the war didn't end at Antietam, the battle really sealed the fate of the Confederacy. Lee's failure to win a decisive victory and carry the war onto Northern turf convinced the European powers not to intervene on the South's behalf.

This tour, a good second-day follow-up to the Antietam–Ziem Vineyards loop (see tour 12), begins at the Jacob Rohrbach Inn on Main Street in Sharpsburg and passes the national cemetery where some five thousand Federal soldiers—almost half of them unknowns—were laid to rest. The tour then enters the battlefield park and visits the Burnside Bridge, turning-point of the battle. Leaving the park, it follows country roads to the Chesapeake & Ohio Canal towpath, which leads along the Potomac River toward Harpers Ferry. That historic town is accessible from the towpath via a pedestrian bridge across the Potomac. The return trip doubles back along the towpath and then enters Sharpsburg by a different route.

0.0 *Leave the Jacob Rohrbach Inn, whose original owner was killed defending his home from Confederate raiders during the Battle of Antietam. If you are not staying at the inn, park on Main Street (MD 34) and proceed east.*

0.5 *To your right is Antietam National Cemetery.*

Most of the Confederate dead are buried elsewhere—some in local churchyards.

0.9 *Turn right on Rodman Avenue (unmarked) into the battlefield park. Follow the road up a hill and down again. Turn left in front of a farmhouse that was there since before the battle, following signs to the Burnside Bridge.*

1.9 *Using the handicapped-access route, bike directly to the historic bridge over Antietam Creek. Otherwise, you will have to bike up a steep hill to the parking lot and walk down a flight of steps.*

From about 9:30 AM on September 17, 1862, Federal troops led by Gen. Ambrose E. Burnside tried to cross this stone arch bridge across Antietam Creek but were continually driven back by about four hundred Georgians. By 1 PM they succeeded, and by late afternoon they had driven the Georgians almost back to Sharpsburg. But then fresh Confederate troops arrived from Harpers Ferry and drove Burnside back to the heights above the bridge that now bears his name. Indecisive as this sounds, it meant that the Battle of Antietam was over. The next day, Lee began withdrawing his forces across the Potomac. Today the hard-fought bridge is a popular spot for picnics and for launching canoes on Antietam Creek. After viewing the bridge, turn back to the intersection by the old farmhouse.

2.4 *Walk your bike down the grassy bank and turn right on New Burnside Bridge Road, which climbs some winding hills.*

4.3 *Turn right on Mills Road.*

6.0 *Turn left on Harpers Ferry Road.*

8.3 *Turn right on Mount Lock Road and follow it downhill to the towpath.*

Visitors stroll the streets of historic Harpers Ferry, site of John Brown's raid.

8.5 *Enter the Chesapeake & Ohio Canal towpath and turn left.*

In the days when the canal was operational—from the 1830s through the 1870s—two mules, led by a mule driver, would tread this path for each boat. Average speed was between 2 and 3 miles per hour.

12.4 *To your left are the ruins of a lock tender's house, which was part of the pay for the job.*

14.1 *Lock your bike and climb the steps to an old truss railroad bridge, which has a safe wooden walkway across the Potomac to Harpers Ferry. Do not use the upstream girder bridge, which still carries trains.*

Stop at the visitors center on Shenandoah Street and pick up a map for a self-guided tour. The arsenal—captured in 1859 by abolitionist John Brown and recaptured by then–U.S. Army officer Robert E. Lee after a bloody fight—is right in front of you after you leave the bridge. Harpers Ferry also has restaurants and rest rooms. After visiting Harpers Ferry, recross the bridge and turn left on the towpath.

22.8 *The towpath crosses Antietam Aqueduct, which carried the canal across Antietam Creek. It's best to walk your bike across because the grass conceals dangerous crevices.*

24.2 *Exit the towpath, walking your bike across the dry, grass-covered canal and across the frontage road. Head up Millers Sawmill Road, which travels through a small settlement and winds up and down some roller-coaster hills.*

25.9 *Turn left on Harpers Ferry Road, which leads into Sharpsburg.*

27.0 *Turn left on Main Street.*

27.2 *Arrive back at Jacob Rohrbach Inn.*

Bicycle Repair Services

Hub City Cycle Center, 35 North Prospect, Hagerstown; 301-797-9877
  No rentals
Potomac Pushbikes, 11 East Potomac Street, Williamsport; 301-582-4747
  Rentals

Reels & Wheels, 17328 Taylors Landing Road, Sharpsburg; 301-432-7281
March to October only

Accommodations

Jacob Rohrbach Inn, 138 West Main Street, Sharpsburg, MD 21782; 301-432-5079
Inn at Antietam, 220 East Main Street, Sharpsburg, MD 21782; 301-432-6601

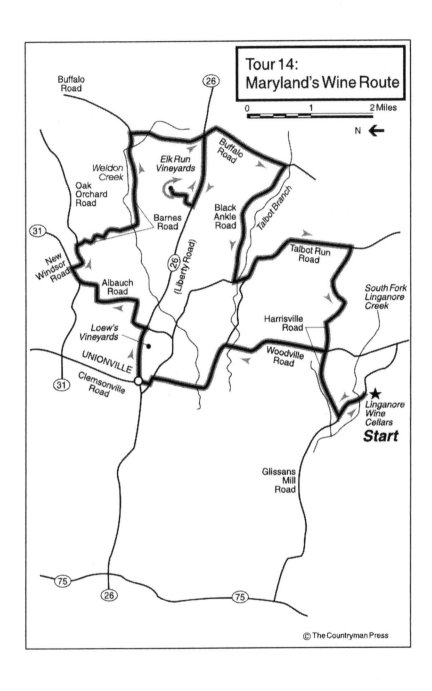

Tour 14:
Maryland's Wine Route

0   1   2 Miles

N

Buffalo Road

Elk Run Vineyards

Buffalo Road

Weldon Creek

Oak Orchard Road

Barnes Road

Black Ankle Road

Talbot Branch

31

New Windsor Road

Albauch Road

(Liberty Road)

26

Talbot Run Road

South Fork Linganore Creek

Loew's Vineyards

Harrisville Road

UNIONVILLE

Woodville Road

31

Clemsonville Road

Linganore Wine Cellars

Start

Glissans Mill Road

75

26

75

© The Countryman Press

14

Maryland's Wine Route

Location: Frederick County
Terrain: Moderately hilly
Road conditions: Paved country roads, most with light traffic
Distance: 23 miles
Highlights: Linganore Winecellars, Loew Vineyards, Elk Run Vineyards

Early Marylanders made wine from whatever berries and fruits they had handy. And, in the seventeenth century, Lord Baltimore tried to import European vines, but they died on the long sea voyage. Catawba grapes were successfully grown and made into wine for many years, but European-style winemaking from vinifera grapes began when a Baltimore Sun correspondent smuggled cuttings of vines out of France during World War II. The state now has about a dozen wineries, producing six hundred thousand bottles a year with total sales of more than $2.5 million.

This tour loops through the rolling farmland of Frederick County near Mount Airy—an area of weathered red barns and small, lively streams—and visits three wineries that offer tours and tastings. It begins at Linganore Winecellars at 13601 Glissans Mill Road in Mount Airy. To reach the winery, take exit 62 from I-70 and head north on MD 75 to Glissans Mill Road. Take Glissans Mill Road east to the winery, which has a large parking lot, picnic grounds, and a wide variety of wines—from dandelion wine to more conventional types.

0.0 From the parking lot, a dirt drive leads down a hill, past a pond.

0.3 Exit the vineyard grounds, turning left on Glissans Mill Road, a country road lined with farms and cattle ranches.

0.8 After crossing a narrow brook, turn right on Harrisville Road, which is unmarked and runs just south of another stream.

1.8 Turn left on Woodville Road, which rolls and winds through farmland and past suburban-type houses.

5.0 At the fork in the gingerbread village of Unionville, bear right on Clemsonville Road.

5.2 At the intersection with Liberty Road (MD 26), turn right.

5.8 At the sign, turn right into Loew Vineyards.

5.9 Leave your bike outside the tasting room and sample some of the offerings of this 4-acre vineyard.

The vineyard's owner is from Austria. Among the wines available are Chardonnay, Seyval, and Cabernet Sauvignon.

6.0 Exit the vineyard grounds and turn right on Liberty Road.

6.2 Crossing the road carefully, turn left on Albauch Road, a hard-packed gravel road that turns right and leads up and down a series of roller-coaster hills.

7.9 Turn right on New Windsor Road (MD 31).

8.1 Turn right on Oak Orchard Road.

8.4 Turn right on Barnes Road, which goes down a hill into a ferny, wooded dell and winds along Weldon Creek.

10.8 Barnes Road ends. Turn right on Buffalo Road, which goes up a hill through woods.

11.9 Turn right on Liberty Road (MD 26).

12.9 Turn right into Elk Run Vineyards, whose tasting room is housed in the summer kitchen of a circa-1750 stone house that served as a tavern—Liberty Tavern on Liberty Road—for travelers trekking between Baltimore and Frederick.

Some of Elk Run's best, prize-winning wines are named for the tavern: Liberty Tavern Reserve Chardonnay and Liberty Tavern Reserve Cabernet Sauvignon. The winery also produces an excellent Gewurztraminer.

13.0 After your tour, leave the winery grounds and turn left on Liberty Road, doubling back.

14.0 Turn right on Buffalo Road, which leads downhill through woods thick with goldfinches and past a lumber mill.

15.4 Make a sharp right onto Black Ankle Road, which is unmarked. This narrow road leads first through woods, along gurgling Talbot Branch, then emerges by fields grazed by Black Angus cattle.

17.5 At the stop sign, turn left.

17.6 Turn left again on Talbot Run Road.

19.6 Turn right on Harrisville Road.

22.4 Turn left on Glissans Mill Road.

23.0 Reenter the Linganore Winecellars grounds.

Bicycle Repair Service

Mount Airy Bicycles, 4540 Old National Pike, Mount Airy; 301-831-5151.
   Rentals

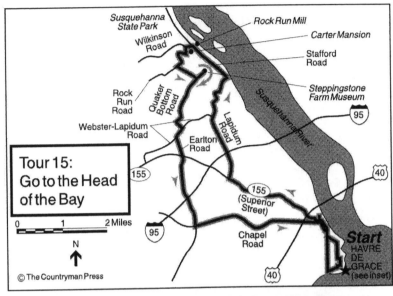

**Tour 15:
Go to the Head
of the Bay**

Susquehanna
State Park

Rock Run Mill

Wilkinson
Road

Carter Mansion

Stafford
Road

Rock
Run
Road

Steppingstone
Farm Museum

Quaker Bottom Road

95

Webster-Lapidum
Road

Lapidum Road

Susquehanna River

Earlton
Road

155

155
(Superior
Street)

40

95

Chapel
Road

Start
HAVRE
DE
GRACE
(see inset)

40

0   1   2 Miles

N

© The Countryman Press

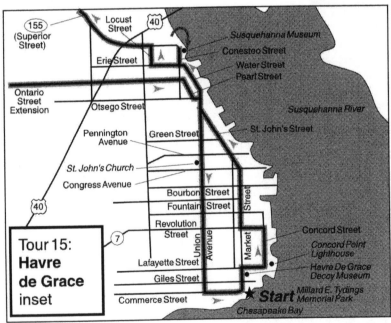

155
(Superior
Street)

Locust
Street

40

Susquehanna Museum

Conesteo Street

Erie Street

Water Street
Pearl Street

Ontario
Street
Extension

Otsego Street

Susquehanna River

Pennington
Avenue

Green Street

St. John's Street

St. John's Church

Congress Avenue

40

Bourbon Street

Fountain Street

**Tour 15:
Havre
de Grace
inset**

7

Revolution
Street

Union Avenue

Market Street

Concord Street

Concord Point
Lighthouse

Lafayette Street

Havre De Grace
Decoy Museum

Giles Street

Commerce Street

★ **Start**

Millard E. Tydings
Memorial Park

Chesapeake Bay

15
Go to the Head of the Bay

Location: *Havre de Grace and surrounding Harford County*
Terrain: *Hilly*
Road conditions: *Paved roads, most with light traffic*
Distance: *17.8 miles*
Highlights: *Historic Havre de Grace, the Concord Point Lighthouse, the Susquehanna & Tidewater Canal and Lockhouse, Susquehanna State Park, the Steppingstone Museum*

Lafayette was not only here—he named the place: harbor of grace. Don't try pronouncing it as Lafayette would have, however. Today, it's "hay-ver-dee-grayce," but it's still a graceful and gracious town at the head of Chesapeake Bay and the mouth of the Susquehanna River. A ferry ran across the Susquehanna from here in the early eighteenth century, and taverns and inns met the needs of travelers going to and from Philadelphia. Later modes of transport, including a canal and the railroad, also enriched the town, economically as well as historically.

This tour begins on the Havre de Grace waterfront (in Tydings Memorial Park at the foot of Union Avenue), visits the old canal lockhouse, travels into the country and along the Susquehanna River, and returns to the starting point via the historic residential district.

0.0 *Exit the park, named for favorite son Senator Millard Tydings, and turn right, continuing along the waterfront on Commerce Street, which immediately turns right and becomes Market Street.*

0.1 *At right, at Giles and Market Streets, is the Havre de Grace Decoy Museum.*

The museum celebrates a local folk art. There is an admission fee.

0.2 *Turn right on Lafayette Street and ride 3 blocks to the Concord Point Lighthouse, the oldest continuously operating lighthouse in the state.*

The 36-foot granite tower, begun in 1826, originally used whale-oil lamps with tin reflectors to warn sailors of the hazardous shoals where the river flows into the bay. It was electrified in 1920. John O'Neill, an Irish immigrant, was the first keeper—a post earned as a reward for heroism on the site during the War of 1812. From a small fort located here, O'Neill fired a single cannon at the British in a vain attempt to stave off an invasion. He was wounded, captured, and scheduled for hanging, but his daughter obtained his release from the British commander, Admiral Cockburn (who later burned the White House). The post was almost hereditary: O'Neills held the job, with only an occasional hiatus, until 1919. The decommissioned lighthouse is now run by a volunteer group, which is in the process of restoring the lighthouse keeper's home across the street. Visitors may climb the winding staircase of the lighthouse on weekend afternoons from May to October. Admission is free.

0.3 *Exiting the lighthouse, turn right on Concord Street, which runs along the waterfront.*

0.5 *Turn left on Revolution Street.*

0.6 *Turn right on Market Street, which has several antiques shops.*

1.0 *Bear left on St. John Street.*

1.4 *St. John Street dead-ends at Union Avenue. Bear right.*

1.5 *After crossing Otsego Street, continue straight, on Water Street.*

At 654 Water Street, across from a rather industrial-looking waterfront, stands Price's Seafood Restaurant, which has excellent crab cakes and soft crabs at reasonable prices.

1.7 *Turn left on Erie Street.*

1.9 *Turn right on Conesteo Street to the Susquehanna Museum, in the lock tender's house at the southern terminus of the Susquehanna & Tidewater Canal.*

Opened in 1839, the Susquehanna & Tidewater Canal ran 45 miles upriver into the rich farmland of Pennsylvania. After a heyday in the 1860s, the canal gradually declined in importance, a victim of competition from the railroads. The lock is still visible, and volunteers conduct tours of the lock tender's house. The museum is open Sunday afternoons from April through October. Admission is free.

Unfortunately, only a small section of the towpath used by the mules is still there, adjacent to the museum. Volunteers dream of resurrecting it one day. Until then, bicyclists have to continue this tour by road. After touring the museum, retrace your path to Erie Street and turn right.

2.3 *Turn right on Locust Street.*

2.4 *Turn left on Superior Street, which becomes MD 155. This is a busy road with a shoulder. It leaves Havre de Grace and climbs a long, winding hill.*

4.4 *Turn right on Lapidum Road, which, after crossing over I-95, turns into a country road that travels mainly downhill.*

6.2 *Lapidum Road enters Susquehanna State Park.*

7.0 *Lapidum Road ends at the Susquehanna River. Turn left on Stafford Road*

There is a boat launch here, and you can see traces of the old canal and of the railroad tracks that displaced it. Stafford Road runs along the wide, island-strewn river.

8.0 *On your right is the restored Rock Run Mill, built near the end of the eighteenth century.*

Corn is ground at the mill for visitors on summer weekends. Take time to stroll along the river and view the remains of a bridge that once crossed it here. Adjacent to the mill is a restored canal tollhouse with an exhibit on the ecology of the river and the Chesapeake Bay.

8.1 *Turn left on Rock Run Road.*

8.2 *The Carter Mansion (left), a magnificent stone house built in 1804 by one of the owners of the mill, is open on summer weekends.*

8.4 *At the intersection with Wilkinson Road, keep left on Rock Run Road, which winds uphill along a stream.*

8.9 *Turn left on Quaker Bottom Road and continue uphill.*

9.5 *Turn left onto the grounds of the Steppingstone Farm Museum.*

The museum is dedicated to preserving the rural arts and crafts of the period from 1880 to 1920. A once-working farm, it includes a blacksmith's shop, a cooper's shop, a potter's shed, a dairy, and many other buildings, with demonstrations in each. The museum is open weekends from May through the first weekend in October, and admission is charged.

After touring the museum and exiting the grounds, continue straight on Quaker Bottom Road.

11.5 *Turn right on Webster-Lapidum Road.*

11.7 *Turn left on Earlton Road.*

13.6 *Turn left on Chapel Road.*

15.9 *Chapel Road crosses the railroad tracks and becomes Ontario Street Extension.*

16.0 *Cross US 40 at the light. Fast-food restaurants are available here. Continue on Ontario Street through an old residential neighborhood of Havre de Grace.*

16.4 *Ontario Street ends. Turn right on Pearl Street.*

16.5 *Turn left on Ostego Street.*

16.6 *Turn right on Union Avenue, lined with antiques shops in this area. Then the shops give way to grand old homes.*

16.8 *On the northwest corner, at the intersection of Union and Green, stands the Aveilhe-Goldsborough house.*

The Aveilhe-Goldsborough house was built by a French émigré in 1801 in the French style. Note the hipped slate roof.

On the northwest corner of Union and Pennington stands the Seneca Mansion, a grand frame Victorian built by a former city mayor. The 22-room structure is an exuberant hodgepodge of turrets, domes, dormers, and bays.

One block farther, at the intersection with Congress Street, stands St. John's Church, built in 1809 in Flemish bond. The Methodist Church, diagonally across the street and built almost a century later, provides a striking contrast to simple St. John's. The imposing church, constructed on local granite, features elaborate arches filled with stained-glass windows. Just to the south of the church are two frame houses, built in a combination of the Queen Anne and Stick styles in the 1880s by Arthur Vosbury—one for his daughter and one for his son.

At the southwest corner of Bourbon and Union is the Spencer-Silver Mansion, now a bed & breakfast inn. This high Victorian stone house was built in 1896 by John Spencer, a foundry owner, and later purchased by Charles Silver, who owned a cannery. At 301 South Union, at the intersection with Fountain Street, stands the Vandiver Inn, a very large Queen Anne cottage with five chimneys. The house was built in 1886 by Murray Vandiver, then mayor of Havre de Grace. In addition to accommodations, the inn also offers excellent dinners.

17.7 Turn left on Commerce Street.

17.8 Enter Tydings Park.

Bicycle Repair Service

PJ's Ski and Sport, Festival at Bel Air Shopping Center, Bel Air; 410-515-0010
No rentals

Accommodations

Vandiver Inn, 301 South Union Avenue, Havre de Grace, MD 21078; 410-939-5200
Spencer-Silver Mansion, 200 South Union Avenue, Havre de Grace, MD 21078; 410-939-1097

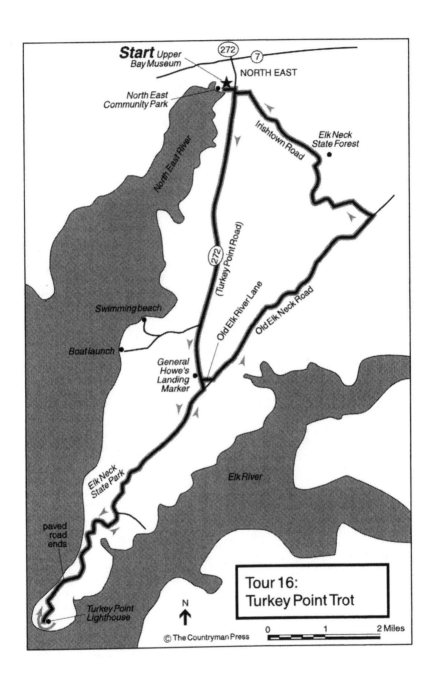

Start Upper Bay Museum

North East Community Park

North East River

Swimming beach

Boat launch

General Howe's Landing Marker

Elk Neck State Park

paved road ends

Turkey Point Lighthouse

272
7

NORTH EAST

Irishtown Road

Elk Neck State Forest

272 (Turkey Point Road)

Old Elk River Lane

Old Elk Neck Road

Elk River

N

Tour 16: Turkey Point Trot

0   1   2 Miles

© The Countryman Press

16
Turkey Point Trot

Location: *Cecil County*
Terrain: *Very hilly*
Road conditions: *Paved roads with seasonal traffic; one short dirt road*
Distance: *27.7 miles*
Highlights: *The Upper Bay Museum, Elk Neck State Park, Turkey Point Lighthouse*

At the top end of Chesapeake Bay, the Northeast and Elk Rivers squeeze out a narrow **V**-shaped peninsula that is called Elk Neck but that ends at Turkey Point. This tour begins at the top of the neck, in North East, a small town just off I-95 equipped with seafood restaurants and antiques shops. The tour leads through wooded parkland to the lighthouse at Turkey Point, on a hundred-foot clay bluff at the confluence of the Elk River and Chesapeake Bay.

One of the chief differences between the Upper Bay region and the Bay country to the south is that the Upper Bay has more hills. For that reason—and because summer weekends bring heavy automobile traffic—this tour is recommended for brisker weather, perhaps during the fall foliage season.

Begin the tour at the Upper Bay Museum, located in North East Community Park, where there is ample parking. The museum, which charges admission, features decoys, boats, and other memorabilia related to fishing—particularly herring fishing—and duck hunting in the area. Note the ice-fishing house.

0.0 *Exit the community park onto Walnut Street.*

0.3 *Turn right on Main Street (MD 272), which becomes Turkey Point Road and leads up and down a series of long, gradual hills.*

Turkey Point Lighthouse towers above Chesapeake Bay atop white clay cliffs.

5.7 *The paved shoulder ends, and the road winds up a hill with farmhouses on either side of the road.*

6.0 *At the top of the hill, look left for a view of farmland rolling down to the Elk River.*

Three hundred British warships landed troops here on August 27, 1877, under the command of General Howe. The force marched up along the Elk River toward Philadelphia and defeated Washington's troops at the Battle of Brandywine on September 11.

6.5 *Turn right at the intersection for the park's swimming beach on the North East River. Turn left to the boat-launch area. To continue the tour, go straight on Turkey Point Road, through parkland covered with hardwoods, pines, ferns, and rhododendrons.*

Paths through the woods on the right lead to yellow-sand beaches.

11.4 *Just past a residential area, the paved road ends. Follow a dirt-and-gravel park road that is rough in spots.*

12.3 *The road ends at the lighthouse, a 35-foot white tower built in 1834, on a rolling green lawn with picnic tables and views of the bay.*

Before the lighthouse was built, mariners, going back to the time of Capt. John Smith, used the white clay bluffs below where the lighthouse now stands as a beacon. Today, signs warn that erosion has made walking along the cliff risky. After a rest stop at the lighthouse, reverse direction and double back on Turkey Point Road.

18.7 *Just past the small white church and the historical marker about General Howe's landing on your left, turn right on Old Elk River Lane, and then make an immediate left onto Old Elk Neck Road, which has marginally fewer hills than Turkey Point Road and much less traffic.*

23.3 *Turn left on Irishtown Road, which skirts Elk Neck State Forest and runs through suburban subdivisions.*

27.3 *Cross MD 272 and ride on the sidewalk, against traffic, for 2 blocks.*

27.4 Turn left on Walnut Street.

27.7 Return to Upper Bay Museum.

Bicycle Repair Service

Pete's Cycle Co., 310 South Main Street, Bel Air; 410-838-8026
  No rentals

Accommodations

North Bay Bed & Breakfast, 9 Sunset Drive, North East, MD 21901;
  410-287-5948

Cabins and Campsites

Elk Neck State Park, 4395 Turkey Point Road, North East, MD 21901;
  410-287-5333

SOUTHERN MARYLAND

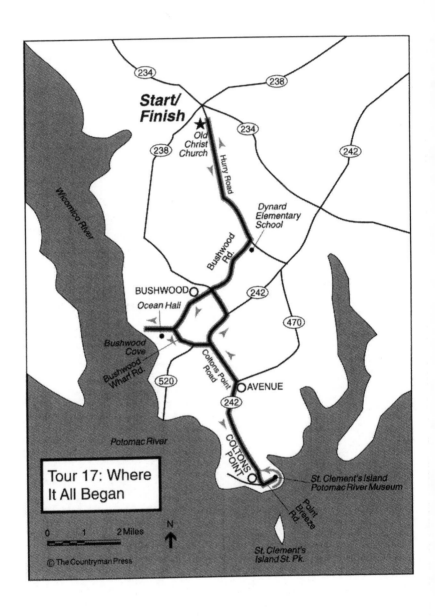

Start/Finish

234

238

234

238

242

Old Christ Church

Hurry Road

Dynard Elementary School

Wicomico River

Bushwood Rd.

BUSHWOOD

242

Ocean Hall

470

Bushwood Cove

Coltons Point Road

Bushwood Wharf Rd.

520

AVENUE

242

Potomac River

COLTONS POINT

Tour 17: Where It All Began

St. Clement's Island Potomac River Museum

Point Breeze Rd.

0   1   2 Miles

N

© The Countryman Press

St. Clement's Island St. Pk.

17
Where It All Began

Location: St. Mary's County
Terrain: Flat with a few hills
Road conditions: Country roads with light traffic
Distance: 26.5 miles
Highlights: Historic Christ Church, Ocean Hall, Bushwood Wharf, St. Clement's Island, St. Clement's Island Potomac River Museum

In early March 1634, Maryland's first white settlers—about two hundred men, women, and children—packed onto two small ships, the Ark and the Dove; sailed up the Potomac River; and landed on a 400-acre island, which they christened St. Clement's. Father Andrew White, one of two Jesuit priests and the group's chronicler, described it as an island replete with heron, cedar, sassafras, and black walnut—all of which are still here. Most of the settlers camped out here while their leaders, headed by Leonard Calvert, went farther upriver and negotiated a deal with the Piscataway tribe for what became St. Mary's City—named for Queen Henrietta Marie, a French Catholic and the wife of King Charles I, who, although head of the Church of England, believed in the principle of religious freedom and gave the land to the Calverts for that purpose.

Every weekend from Memorial Day through October and also on Maryland Day, March 25, you can visit the island where Maryland began—now shrunken to some 60 acres—via a water taxi from the St. Clement's Island Potomac River Museum, whose exhibits explain the major figures in Maryland's early history as well as the ecology of the Potomac watershed. The museum and the island are the focus of this tour to where Maryland, as we know it, began. The tour actually begins at a site from a more recent time period in the state's history, at Christ Church in Chaptico, built in 1736, although established as a parish in

1692—shortly after the Catholic Calverts lost control of the colony and religious freedom effectively ended. After pausing at the lovely old church and its cemetery, the tour takes off, following country roads past corn and soybean fields to one of the oldest extant houses in Maryland, Ocean Hall, built circa 1703. After a stop at Bushwood Wharf, the tour continues backward in history to the 1634 St. Clement's landing.

Christ Church is on MD 238, just south of the intersection of MD 234 in Chaptico. There is a parking lot where you can leave your car.

0.0 Begin the tour at historic Christ Church.

Take a few moments to soak in the history of this lovely old church, which may have been designed by the famed English architect Sir Christopher Wren. The weathered redbrick exterior, arranged in Flemish bond, encloses a simple but elegant nave whose high arched ceiling rests on intricately carved columns. Stained-glass windows filter sunlight and cast color on the simple white interior. The scene was not always so peaceful, however. During the War of 1812, the British Navy landed at Chaptico and wreaked havoc on the church. According to a contemporary account, "they picked their stolen geese in the church, dashed the pipes of the organ on the pavement, opened coffins, stirred the bones about with their hands in search of hidden treasures." The church is on the National Register of Historic Places.

After viewing the church and cemetery, walk around to the left of the church and enter Hurry Road, turning right. You will go up a small hill, through woods, and alongside fields of soybeans.

4.0 At Dynard Elementary School, turn right onto Bushwood Road.

5.7 Cross MD 238 and continue on Bushwood Road.

The Bushwood Post Office, on your right just past the intersection, has a porch with an inviting rocking chair. The road continues past farms and through woods.

7.3 At the V, continue straight ahead.

On your left, surrounded by fields, stands Ocean Hall, a privately owned home that dates from circa 1703. The brick house with its steep gabled roof is typical of the early tidewater Maryland plantation homes. Continue straight ahead to Bushwood Wharf, once part of bustling Port Wicomico, which served as a steamboat land-

Bushwood Wharf, once a bustling steamboat stop, now serves only a small fleet of work and pleasure boats.

ing and from which tobacco was shipped from colonial times until 1930. All that remains is a general store and a wharf serving pleasure and work boats.

7.6 *After drinking in the view of the broad Wicomico River, turn around at the end of the road and retrace your route until you come to the V again.*

8.0. *At the V, bear right on Bushwood Wharf Road, which leads through tobacco and corn fields.*

9.3 *Turn right on MD 242, heading south.*

10.7 *The small settlement of Avenue has food shops. At the crossroads, continue on MD 242, bearing right.*

11.9 *The Avenue General Store is on your left.*

13.8 *At the Coltons Point Post Office, turn left on Point Breeze Road, following the signs to the St. Clement's Island Potomac River Museum.*

14.0 *Turn right into the museum. There are benches where you can lock your bike while you visit the museum and the island. After your visit, leave the museum and turn left on Point Breeze Road.*

The museum is open daily from March 25 through September, weekdays from 9 AM to 5 PM and weekends from noon to 5 PM. From October 1 through March 24, it's open Wednesday through Sunday from noon to 4 PM. There is an admission fee for adults. The water taxi to the island is available weekends from Memorial Day through October from 12:30 to 2:30 PM. A very pleasant walking trail from the dock leads past outdoor exhibits about the island and its history to a replica of the cross erected by the settlers on March 25, 1634, now celebrated as Maryland Day. Picnic tables are available both on the island and on the museum grounds.

14.2 *Turn right on MD 242.*

17.3 *In the settlement of Avenue, bear left at the crossroads, continuing on MD 242.*

19.6 *At the intersection, bear left on MD 238.*

20.8 *Turn right on Bushwood Road.*

22.5 At Dynard Elementary School, turn left on Hurry Road.

26.5 Arrive back at Christ Church.

Bicycle Repair Service

Mike's Bike Shop, 21310-C Great Mills Road, Lexington Park; 301-863-7887
No rentals

Accommodations

Enfields Bed and Breakfast, Avenue, MD 20609; 301-769-4755

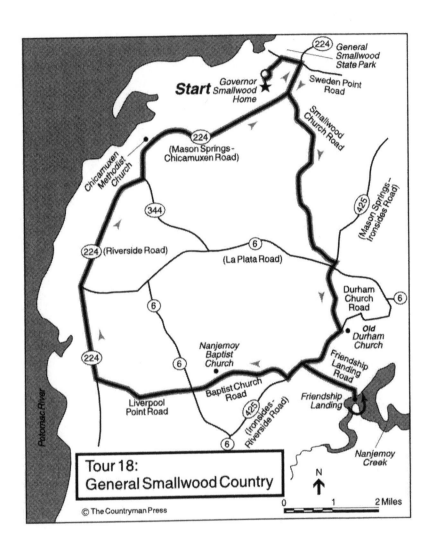

Start Governor Smallwood Home

General Smallwood State Park

Sweden Point Road

224

Smallwood Church Road

224 (Mason Springs-Chicamuxen Road)

Chicamuxen Methodist Church

344

425 (Mason Springs-Ironsides Road)

224 (Riverside Road)

6 (La Plata Road)

6

Durham Church Road

6

224

6

Old Durham Church

Nanjemoy Baptist Church

Friendship Landing Road

6

Baptist Church Road

425 (Ironsides-Riverside Road)

Friendship Landing

Liverpool Point Road

6

Nanjemoy Creek

Potomac River

Tour 18: General Smallwood Country

© The Countryman Press

N

0   1   2 Miles

18
General Smallwood Country

Location: *Charles County*
Terrain: *Rolling*
Road conditions: *Paved roads with light traffic*
Distance: *26.5 miles*
Highlights: *Smallwood State Park, Old Durham Church, Nanjemoy Creek, Chicamuxen Methodist Church*

Gen. William Smallwood probably saved George Washington at the Battle of Long Island by covering the Continental Army's retreat to Brooklyn. He lost 256 men in the process but gained for Maryland the title of The Old Line State for the way his troops held the line. Smallwood served as Maryland's governor from 1785 to 1788, then retired to his plantation, which is now a state park bearing his name. The tour starts at this restored, small-but-elegant plantation home and travels through rolling farmland and woods to the Old Durham Church, to which parishioner Smallwood once contributed 3,000 pounds of tobacco to pay for a new roof. After a picnic stop at a boat-launching area and fishing dock on picturesque Nanjemoy Creek, the route traverses swampland and farms and loops back to the park.

To reach the park from the Washington Beltway, take MD 210 south to the intersection with MD 225. Take MD 225 east to the intersection with MD 224. Take MD 224 south to the park. There is an admission charge, per car.

0.0 *From the restored home and grave of General Smallwood, follow the signs to the park exit.*

0.5 *Continue up a small hill on Sweden Point Road.*

0.8 *Turn right on Mason Springs–Chicamuxen Road (MD 224), which goes down a hill and up another one.*

The time for services was set by this sundial at Old Durham Church.

1.4 Turn left on Smallwood Church Road, a country byway through woods and fields.

5.6 At the intersection, turn right on Mason Springs–Ironsides Road (MD 425) and follow it across MD 6.

7.0 To your left stands Old Durham Church, founded in 1692.

The rather plain, boxy brick church itself dates from 1732 and was restored two hundred years later in honor of Smallwood, a vestryman. Another Smallwood connection: The bell tower is made of bricks from the ruins of the home of Smallwood's sister. A sundial in front of the church determined the time for beginning Sunday services, and the churchyard holds graves dating as far back as 1690.

8.2 Turn left on Friendship Landing Road.

This road leads to a public area on the banks of marshy Nanjemoy Creek, an excellent place to watch great blue herons.

9.8 After a stop by the creek, reverse direction along Friendship Landing Road.

11.4 Turn left on Ironsides–Riverside Road (MD 425).

12.0 At the bottom of a hill, turn right on Baptist Church Road.

13.7 After crossing a swamp bright with water lilies and loud with the croaking of frogs, the road climbs a small rise to the Nanjemoy Baptist Church, on your right.

In 1790 four men crossed the Potomac from Virginia to preach in this area, and five years later a church was built on this site. The present white frame church dates from the nineteenth century.

14.2 After crossing MD 6, Baptist Church Road becomes Liverpool Point Road.

15.8 The small store to your right sells snacks and cold drinks.

16.2 Turn right on Riverside Road (MD 224), which rolls up and down hills, crossing swamps and thick woods.

21.1 At the junction with MD 344, continue on MD 224, turning left onto what becomes Mason Springs–Chicamuxen Road.

22.5 The white frame Chicamuxen Methodist Church, to your left, served as headquarters for Gen. Joseph Hooker.

Hooker's twelve thousand troops camped along the Potomac near here from October 1861 until March 1862. The general's main claim to fame comes from his setting aside a red-light district in wartime Washington, thus lending his name to practitioners of the world's oldest profession.

25.7 *Turn left on Sweden Point Road and follow it into Smallwood State Park.*

26.5 *Arrive at the parking lot for the Smallwood home.*

Bicycle Repair Service

Mike's Bikes, Pinefield Shopping Center, US 301 and Mattawoman-Beantown Road, Waldorf; 301-870-6600
No rentals

19

On the Trail of John Wilkes Booth

Location: *Charles County*
Terrain: *Rolling*
Road conditions: *Paved roads with light traffic*
Distance: *23.7 miles*
Highlights: *Dr. Mudd's House, St. Mary's Church and Cemetery, Trinity Episcopal Church, Zekiah Swamp, crab restaurants on the Potomac at Pope's Creek*

Shouting "Sic semper tyrannis" ("so always to tyrants"), John Wilkes Booth shot President Abraham Lincoln and jumped to the stage of Ford's Theater, breaking his leg. Early the next morning, on his way to Confederate Virginia, he stopped at the farm of a country doctor, Samuel Mudd, who set Booth's leg. Was Mudd part of the conspiracy to kill Lincoln or just a physician following the Hippocratic oath? The guides at the restored farmhouse, some of whom are descendants of Dr. Mudd, make a strong case for the good doctor's innocence. Mudd was convicted by a military court of conspiracy in the assassination and sentenced to life imprisonment in Fort Jefferson in the Dry Tortugas. He was pardoned for his heroic service during a yellow fever epidemic, but his descendants and their supporters are trying to have the doctor exonerated and the Mudd name cleared.

This tour begins at Dr. Mudd's house, at the intersection of MD 382 and 232, west of Waldorf. After a visit to the house, which contains furniture made by Dr. Mudd in prison as well as the sofa on which John Wilkes Booth rested, the tour visits Dr. Mudd's grave, at the church where he first met Booth, and follows a rough approximation of Booth's escape route from Mudd's farm to the Potomac. The chief differences are that it skirts, rather than traverses, the Zekiah Swamp and that it

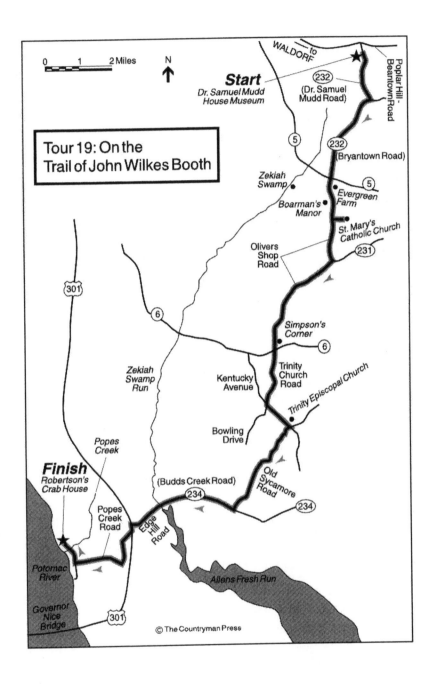

has a happier ending: Instead of crossing the Potomac and being shot in a Virginia barn, like Booth, you can end the tour eating crabs at Pope's Creek, near where Booth was ferried across the river.

0.0 *Leave Dr. Mudd's house and turn right at the end of the drive onto MD 232 (called Dr. Mudd Road at this point and then becoming Bryantown Road).*

1.7 *After climbing a small hill, Bryantown Road bears right at the fork, traversing fields of corn, soybeans, and tobacco.*

4.6 *After crossing MD 5, a four-lane highway, MD 232 becomes Olivers Shop Road.*

4.7 *Evergreen Farm, to your left, was built circa 1871.*

4.9 *To your right stands Boarman's Manor, constructed beginning in 1674 and part of an original tract of 3,333 acres granted in that year to William Boarman by Lord Baltimore.*

5.9 *Turn left into St. Mary's Catholic Church, a redbrick structure that replaced an earlier Jesuit chapel.*

Built in 1848, the church was relatively new when Samuel Mudd, a Roman Catholic, met John Wilkes Booth here after Mass, brought him home to Sunday dinner, and sold him a horse. The two later met in Washington, over drinks, when Dr. Mudd went to the city to buy Christmas presents. Still, Mudd and his wife denied recognizing Booth when he came to the house after shooting Lincoln, because Booth was disguised with stage makeup. They also claimed not to know of the assassination until after Booth had left their home, on horseback. Booth's fellow conspirator had tried to rent a carriage to make the journey easier, but Mudd's neighbors, most of them devout Catholics and parishioners of St. Mary's, refused because they needed their carriages to get to church the next day, Easter Sunday. Dr. Mudd, who died in 1883, lies buried here, shaded by cedars and oaks and surrounded by many other Mudds.

6.3 *Exit the church grounds and turn left on Olivers Shop Road.*

11.0 *Simpson's Corner, to your left, has cold drinks, snacks, and a rest room. Just past the store, Olivers Shop Road crosses MD 6 and becomes Trinity Church Road.*

12.7 *At the intersection of Bowling Drive and Kentucky Avenue, bear left, continuing on Trinity Church Road.*

13.1 *The road crosses Gilbert Swamp Run, then climbs a hill.*

13.6 *To your left is Trinity Episcopal Church.*

Trinity's Flemish bond brick walls were erected in 1793. Later, the walls were added in order to make room for pointed-arch windows. The churchyard contains graves of Revolutionary War soldiers. Just across Trinity Church Road from the church, turn right on Old Sycamore Road, which winds past several fine examples of Maryland tobacco barns, with slats that open to let in air to dry the tobacco.

16.8 *Turn right on Budd's Creek Road, which is sometimes busy and has a shoulder.*

19.0 *The road crosses Allens Fresh Run.*

Allens Fresh Run carries the waters of Zekiah Swamp to the Potomac, cutting a meandering course through marshland that shelters heron and osprey and is adorned with marsh mallow, a white flower related to the hibiscus.

20.3 *After climbing a winding hill, Budd's Creek Road ends at US 301. Cross the highway at the light and turn left, riding on the shoulder of US 301.*

20.7 *Turn right on Edge Hill Road, which winds through woods and past farmhouses.*

21.6 *Turn right on Pope's Creek Road, passing large tobacco farms.*

23.1 *The road curves to the right, runs through woods, and emerges at the point where Pope's Creek runs into the wide Potomac River.*

23.7 *Robertson's Crab House (left) is one of three Pope's Creek restaurants specializing in hard crabs, served with a dipping sauce of vinegar and Old Bay seasoning.*

Long before the Europeans came to Maryland, Indians gathered here to eat oysters, heaping the shells in piles as high as 15 feet. From the restaurants, or from the Potomac shore, look south to the Governor Nice Bridge across the Potomac—which, of course,

A docent welcomes visitors to the home of Dr. Samuel Mudd, who set the broken leg of President Lincoln's assassin, John Wilkes Booth.

wasn't there when John Wilkes Booth needed to get to the other side.

Bicycle Repair Service

Mike's Bikes, Pinefield Shopping Center, US 301 and Mattawoman-Beantown Road, Waldorf; 301-870-6600
No rentals

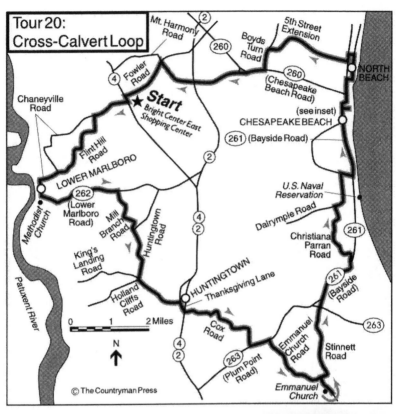

Tour 20:
Cross-Calvert Loop

Mt. Harmony Road
Boyds Turn Road
5th Street Extension
260
Fowler Road
260 (Chesapeake Beach Road)
NORTH BEACH
Chaneyville Road
★ Start
Bright Center East Shopping Center
(see inset)
CHESAPEAKE BEACH
Flint Hill Road
261 (Bayside Road)
LOWER MARLBORO
U.S. Naval Reservation
Methodist Church
262 (Lower Marlboro Road)
Mill Branch Road
Huntingtown Road
Dairymple Road
Christiana Parran Road
261
King's Landing Road
HUNTINGTOWN
Thanksgiving Lane
261 (Bayside Road)
Patuxent River
Holland Cliffs Road
263
0   1   2 Miles
Cox Road
Emmanuel Church Road
Stinnett Road
N
263 (Plum Point Road)
Emmanuel Church
© The Countryman Press

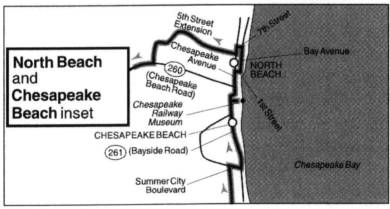

5th Street Extension
7th Street
Chesapeake Avenue
Bay Avenue
North Beach and Chesapeake Beach inset
260 (Chesapeake Beach Road)
NORTH BEACH
Chesapeake Railway Museum
1st Street
CHESAPEAKE BEACH
261 (Bayside Road)
Chesapeake Bay
Summer City Boulevard

20
Cross-Calvert Loop

Location: *Calvert County*
Terrain: *Hilly*
Road conditions: *Paved roads with light to moderate traffic.*
Distance: *33.6 miles*
Highlights: *Historic Lower Marlboro, the Chesapeake Beach Railway Museum, North Beach*

Calvert County, named for Maryland's founding family, is a peninsula bounded by the Patuxent River on the west and Chesapeake Bay on the east. The rural county remains surprisingly close to the way it was when the first settlers came in the seventeenth century—although the tobacco farms that cover its rolling hills are slowly but inexorably being replaced by housing developments.

This tour begins on the ridge between the two bodies of water, on MD 4, which runs in almost a straight line from Calvert's northern border to its southern tip. After a swoop down to the Patuxent and the historic port of Lower Marlboro, the tour takes country roads back across the county and rides along the Chesapeake to the early-twentieth-century summer colonies of Chesapeake Beach and North Beach, which offer opportunities for eating and antiquing. The starting place is Bright Center East shopping center on MD 4 at Chaneyville Road, just south of the Calvert County tourist information center.

0.0 *Cross MD 4 at the light and head west on Chaneyville Road, which goes downhill, through tobacco country.*

0.9 *Just past Northern High School, turn left on Flint Hill Road, which cuts through woods and farmland.*

3.0 *Flint Hill Road rejoins Chaneyville Road. Go straight after the stop sign.*

Tobacco dries in a Calvert County barn.

3.5 *Chaneyville Road curves to the left, following the shore of the Patuxent River.*

Watch for herons flying out of the marshes on the other side of the river.

3.9 *On your left, across the field, stands Patuxent River Manor.*

The manor is an elegantly simple brick house built circa 1744 by Malcolm Graham. The original paneling from the house is now at the Winterthur Museum in Delaware.

4.0 *To your right is the Harbormaster's House, which serves as a reminder of the historic past of the settlement of Lower Marlboro.*

Originally called Coxtown after two early settlers, the town was renamed to honor the Duke of Marlborough after the Battle of Blenheim in 1704. By the mid-eighteenth century it was a thriving port-of-entry, with warehouses, stores, a mill, a racetrack, and many stately homes. Later the river silted up with topsoil, and other ports took away the town's business. Turn right at the Harbormaster's House and follow Lower Marlboro Road down to the public dock. Until the 1930s steamboats called here to take passengers and goods to and from Baltimore.

4.1 *Leave the public dock and go back up the hill to the intersection.*

4.2 *Turn right on Lower Marlboro Lane for a brief tour of the village.*

A 1913 cyclone destroyed many of the old homes, and most date from the decade following that event. The white frame house at the right, across the road from the Methodist churchyard, dates from about 1750, however.

4.4 *After returning to the intersection, turn right on Lower Marlboro Road (MD 262), which climbs a gradual hill, then descends and crosses wooded Mill Branch.*

6.7 *Turn right on Mill Branch Road, which runs through woods and tobacco fields.*

Early Marylanders used tobacco as currency, and tobacco is still an important cash crop in this area. The crop is harvested in late

August and early September and hung in barns open to the air for drying. In the winter or early spring the dried tobacco is stripped and sent to auction houses.

7.4 *At the intersection with Smoky Road, bear left on Mill Branch Road.*

8.0 *Mill Branch Road joins Huntingtown Road. Keep right on Huntingtown Road, which goes down a hill, past a small duck pond, then up a hill, through a suburban development.*

9.4 *At the intersection with Holland Cliffs Road and King's Landing Road, turn left after the stop sign and continue on Huntingtown Road.*

10.1 *At the intersection with MD 521, keep straight on Huntingtown Road (MD 521 E).*

10.6 *Turn right on Thanksgiving Lane and follow it to the blinker light at the intersection with MD 2-4. Cross the highway and continue on Cox Road, which goes through still more tobacco country.*

13.1 *Cox Road ends at Plum Point Road. Turn left on Plum Point Road, which is sometimes busy but has a shoulder.*

13.6 *Turn right on Emmanuel Church Road, a country byway with some serious horse farms.*

15.5 *Emmanuel Church Road curves to the right. Follow it to its namesake, Emmanuel Church.*

Emmanuel Church is a lovely fieldstone-and-slate country church built between 1869 and 1901. Among the boxwoods in the churchyard are some appealing Victorian statues of angels.

After visiting the church, double back on Emmanuel Church Road to the intersection with Stinnett Road.

16.4 *Turn right on Stinnett Road, a hilly road through woods and residential areas.*

18.5 *At the intersection with MD 263 and MD 261, turn right on MD 261 N (Bayside Road), riding on the shoulder.*

19.9 *Turn right on Christiana Parran Road.*

21.8 *Christiana Parran Road ends. Turn right on Dalrymple Road, which is unmarked at this point, and follow it past a U.S. Naval Reservation.*

22.8 *Turn right on Summer City Boulevard, which cuts through a vintage cottage colony.*

23.2 *At the stop sign, turn left on MD 261, keeping to the shoulder as it goes up and down a series of roller-coaster hills. Watch for views of the bay to your right.*

25.0 *Turn right on Mears Avenue.*

25.1 *To your right is the Chesapeake Beach Railway Museum.*

The museum is a relic of the days when the shore of Chesapeake Bay was "the beach" for people from Baltimore and Washington and when the train was the way to get there. Otto Mears, an independent short-line railroad builder from Colorado, built a grand resort here in the 1890s, complete with beachfront hotels, a racetrack, a casino, bathhouses, and a boardwalk with rides and restaurants. Some people arrived by steamer, at the mile-long pier, and others took the train, called the Honeysuckle Special, and arrived right here, at the station. The restored station houses memorabilia of the old resort and of the railway. Across the parking lot from the museum is the Rod N Reel Restaurant, which offers excellent seafood, views of the bay, and a small beach and pier. After a sojourn here, double back on Mears Avenue.

25.2 *Turn right on Bayside Avenue (MD 261) and follow it through the intersection with MD 260.*

26.1 *Turn right on First Street, in the town of North Beach.*

26.2 *Turn left on Bay Avenue, which runs along the water, past the public beach and pier.*

26.6 *At the corner of Bay Avenue and Seventh Street stands Nice 'N Fleazy Antiques. Behind it is Elvira's Antiques. Turn left on Seventh Street, where two more antiques shops are on your left in the first block.*

26.7 *Turn left on Chesapeake Avenue.*

26.8 *Turn right on Fifth Street, which goes past summer cottages* built in the 1920s and earlier, and then climbs a hill and becomes the Fifth Street Extension.

29.0 Turn left on Boyds Turn Road.

29.5 Turn right on MD 260, riding on the shoulder.

29.9 At the intersection at the top of the hill, turn left on Mount Harmony Road.

31.3 Mount Harmony Road crosses MD 2 and continues.

32.3 Take a sharp left on Fowler Road, which climbs some mild hills and passes several housing developments.

33.6 Turn left into the shopping-center parking lot.

Bicycle Repair Service

4 X-Treem Sports, 3865 Old Town Road, Huntingtown; 410-257-7858
  No rentals

EASTERN SHORE

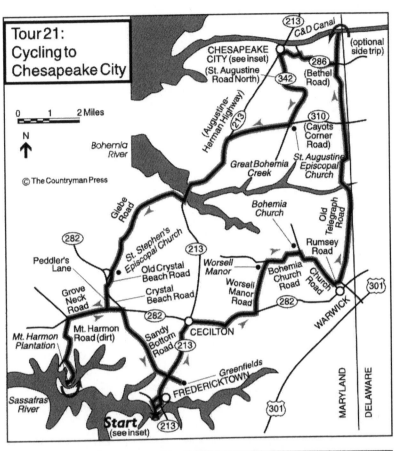

Tour 21: Cycling to Chesapeake City

0   1   2 Miles

N

© The Countryman Press

C&D Canal — 213

CHESAPEAKE CITY (see inset) (St. Augustine Road North) — 342 — 213

(optional side trip)

286 (Bethel Road)

(Augustine-Herman Highway) 213

310 (Cayots Corner Road)

Bohemia River

Great Bohemia Creek

St. Augustine Episcopal Church

Bohemia Church

Old Telegraph Road

Glebe Road

282

St. Stephen's Episcopal Church

213

Rumsey Road

Peddler's Lane

Old Crystal Beach Road

Worsell Manor

Bohemia Church Road

Church Road

301

Grove Neck Road

Crystal Beach Road

Worsell Manor Road

282

WARWICK

Mt. Harmon Plantation

Mt. Harmon Road (dirt)

282

Sandy Bottom Road

CECILTON

213

MARYLAND

DELAWARE

Sassafras River

Greenfields

FREDERICKTOWN

301

Start (see inset) — 213

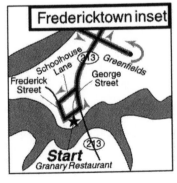

Fredericktown inset

Greenfields

Schoolhouse Lane — 213

George Street

Frederick Street

Start Granary Restaurant — 213

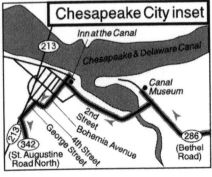

Chesapeake City inset

Inn at the Canal

213

Chesapeake & Delaware Canal

Canal Museum

2nd Street

Bohemia Avenue

4th Street

213 — 342 (St. Augustine Road North)

George Street

286 (Bethel Road)

21
Cycling to Chesapeake City

Location: *Cecil County*
Terrain: *Flat to rolling*
Road conditions: *Mainly paved roads with light traffic*
Distance: *45 miles*
Highlights: *Old Bohemia Church, restored Chesapeake City on the Chesapeake & Delaware Canal, Mount Harmon Plantation*

The Chesapeake & Delaware Canal, conceived in 1661, begun in 1801, opened in 1829, and modernized in 1962, shortens the water route between Baltimore and Philadelphia by almost 300 miles. The "C&D" is also the raison d'être for the bustling, busy canal town at its western terminus, Chesapeake City, an excellent cycling destination with comfortable inns, good food, a museum, and a perfect vantage point for watching both commercial and pleasure craft sail by. Although it would certainly be feasible to complete this tour in one day, there are so many things to see on the way to Chesapeake City, as well as after arriving, that an overnight is suggested at one of the restored bed & breakfast inns in the historic district.

The tour begins at the Granary Restaurant in Fredericktown, a yachting center on the Sassafras River. To get there from the Washington, Baltimore, or Annapolis areas, cross the Bay Bridge and follow US 301 to the junction with MD 213, following 213 north to Georgetown and across the Sassafras River to Fredericktown. As soon as you cross the river, make the first left and follow George Street to the Granary. This is a great place to begin and/or end your journey with some Maryland crab soup or other local specialty.

139

0.0 *Exit the parking lot, heading east along George Street, which is lined with marinas.*

0.3 *Cross MD 213 (Augustine Herman Highway) and turn left, riding on the shoulder up a hill.*

2.0 *In the midst of a field sown with soybeans stands Greenfields, a well-preserved eighteenth-century brick mansion. The house is private, but a 0.4-mile ride up the drive leads to an antiques shop in the barn.*

2.8 *Exit the drive and continue north on MD 213.*

3.8 *Turn right on Main Street (MD 282) in the center of the small settlement of Cecilton.*

6.0 *Turn left on Worsell Manor Road.*

This road is a pleasant country byway that probably looks much as it did to George Washington, who came this way in 1773 to take his stepson to Kings College (later Columbia) in New York.

7.4 *On your left is Worsell Manor, the home of prominent Marylander Daniel Charles Heath; George Washington slept here.*

7.6 *Turn right on Bohemia Church Road.*

8.8 *Turn left into the church grounds.*

9.0 *Park your bike and explore the grounds of this beautiful brick church, built circa 1790 on a rise above the Little Bohemia River.*

The river, the church, and many other things hereabouts derive their names from the Prague birthplace of Augustine Herman, who obtained a vast tract of land here from the Calverts in 1662 in return for making an "exact mapp" of Maryland and Virginia, a task that took 10 years to complete. The real name of the church is St. Francis Xavier, and it was built by Jesuits, many of whom are buried here. When Roman Catholic schools were outlawed in Maryland during the religious strife of the 1700s, a clandestine academy was established here, whose students included America's first Catholic archbishop and a signer of the Declaration of Independence, both members of the Carroll family.

The church is open the third Sunday of the month from June

Old Bohemia Church bears the name of the homeland of Augustine Herman, who mapped the area in return for land.

through September. At other times, you can admire the old boxwood, eat the wild figs growing in the yard, and pay homage at the grave of Kitty Knight, a heroine of the War of 1812. When the British tried to burn her house, she kept putting out the fire with a broom. The British finally gave up, and her house still stands in nearby Georgetown and serves as an inn.

9.2 *Exit the church grounds. Bohemia Church Road turns right here and continues as Church Road.*

10.7 *Turn right on Rumsey Road in the town of Warwick.*

This road is named for James Rumsey, born near here, who demonstrated a working steamboat on the Potomac River 20 years before Robert Fulton's better-known trial run.

10.9 *Turn left on Old Telegraph Road, a long straightaway through endearingly flat farm country.*

14.0 *Old Telegraph Road veers left to cross Great Bohemia Creek, then climbs a hill and travels through rolling countryside filled with horse farms.*

18.1 *Turn left on Bethel Road.*

For a preview of the C&D Canal, continue on Old Telegraph Road until it ends on a bluff with a sweeping view of the waterway. Don't try to ride on the sand road along the canal. It's hard on bikes, and the gate at the Chesapeake City end may be locked. Instead, return to Bethel Road, having added 1.8 miles to the trip.

21.1 *On your right is a museum dedicated to the history of the canal.*

There is also a pumphouse, which houses a waterwheel once used to pump water back into the canal to replace the water lost when a ship went through the lock. The modernized canal has no locks, but the Army Corps of Engineers operates out of the same building, keeping watch on canal traffic.

After visiting the museum, turn right on Second Street, which leads into downtown Chesapeake City.

21.6 *Turn right on Bohemia Avenue, the main street of this charmingly preserved and restored canal town. To leave town and*

start the return trip, take Bohemia Avenue away from the canal.

The Inn at the Canal is at 104 Bohemia Avenue. Across the street is the Bayard House, an excellent restaurant. The street also holds several antiques shops.

21.8 *Turn right on Fourth Street.*

Dead ahead of you looms the enormous bridge that overshadows Chesapeake City, high enough to let the big ships pass underneath. This one was built in 1949 after a tanker demolished one that wasn't quite tall enough.

21.9 *Turn left on George Street, which runs parallel to the bridge above.*

22.0 *Turn left on St. Augustine Road North (MD 342), which runs through race-horse-farm country.*

24.8 *Cross Cayots Corner Road (MD 310) and enter the grounds of St. Augustine Episcopal Church.*

The church was built in 1838 to replace an earlier structure. The large churchyard holds some Duponts and also one Henry Craig who, at his death in 1861, requested that he be buried behind a brick wall with one brick left out so he could escape the devil. The hole has been plugged up, but the marble atop the grave is split, so maybe Craig had his way after all.

After leaving the church grounds, turn left on Cayots Corner Road (MD 310).

26.7 *To your right a historical marker notes that the land hereabouts was once inhabited by the Labadists, a commune of followers of a seventeenth-century French mystic.*

27.0 *Turn left on MD 213 (Augustine Herman Highway), which has a paved shoulder.*

29.4 *After crossing the Bohemia River, turn right on Glebe Road, which runs through a small waterfront community and then turns left.*

30.2 *A general store is on the left.*

33.5 *St. Stephen's Episcopal Church, to your left, dates from 1873.*

At the church, turn left on Old Crystal Beach Road and continue in the same direction after this turns into Crystal Beach Road.

33.9 *At the V go straight onto Peddler's Lane. An old blacksmith shop near the intersection sells antiques.*

34.3 *Turn right on Grove Neck Road.*

35.6 *Turn left onto Mount Harmon Road.*

The road is a dirt lane, canopied by Osage orange trees, that leads to Mount Harmon Plantation, a Georgian manor house built in 1730 (admission fee). Watch for deer crossing the lane.

37.5 *The lane ends at the manor house, which is surrounded by boxwood gardens that lead the eye down to the Sassafras River, where ships called to take away tobacco grown at Mount Harmon.*

39.5 *After exiting the plantation grounds, turn right on Grove Neck Road.*

41.0 *Turn right on Sandy Bottom Road, which goes down a hill and then up another.*

44.1 *Turn right on MD 213 (Augustine Herman Highway).*

44.7 *Turn right on Schoolhouse Lane.*

44.9 *Turn left on Frederick Street.*

45.0 *Enter the parking lot of the Granary Restaurant.*

Bicycle Repair Service

Bikework, 208 South Cross Street, Chestertown; 410-778-6940
No rentals

Accommodations

Inn at the Canal, 104 Bohemia Avenue, Chesapeake City, MD 21915; 410-885-5995

22
Inn to Inn on the Lower Shore

Location: Worcester County
Terrain: Flat
Road conditions: Paved roads with light traffic; paved trail on
  Assateague Island
Distance: 94.9 miles
Highlights: Historic Snow Hill, Chincoteague Bay, Berlin, the wild ponies
  of Assateague Island, the Nassawango Iron Furnace and Furnace
  Town, Milburn Landing State Park on the Pocomoke River

The lower Eastern Shore of Maryland is a cyclist's dream: It's almost total-
ly flat. It also has great scenery, much preserved history, and bicycle-
friendly inns. Some of these hotels and bed & breakfasts have joined
together to provide special services to cyclists. For a per-person daily
fee you get accommodations, breakfast, dinner, transport of your luggage
to the next member inn, and a map for a self-guided tour. Or you can
arrange your own tour and carry your own luggage.

This tour begins at the River House Inn in Snow Hill; swoops down
to the Public Landing on Chincoteague Bay; leads through chicken-
farm country to historic Berlin; continues to Assateague Island, where
wild ponies graze on salt marsh and run by the Atlantic Ocean; and doubles back to Berlin's restored Atlantic Hotel. The second day of the tour
crisscrosses the Pocomoke River and Nassawango Creek, visits an old
iron furnace and restored town, and brings you back to Snow Hill.

This tour is a shorter adaptation (with the addition of a side trip to
Assateague Island) of Viewtrail 100, a well-marked 100-mile tour
mapped out by Worcester County.

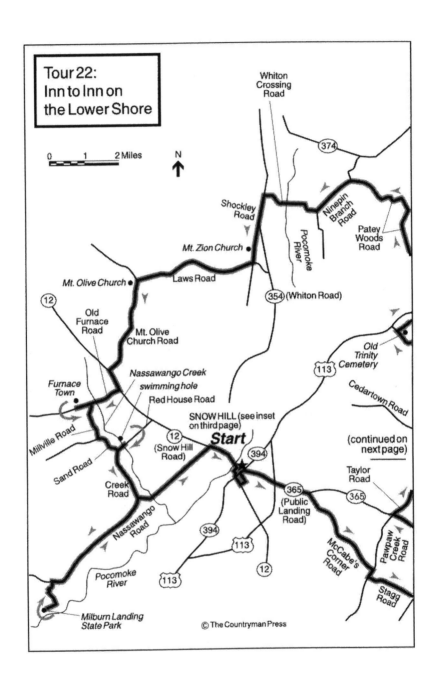

Tour 22:
Inn to Inn on
the Lower Shore

0   1   2 Miles

N

Whiton
Crossing
Road

374

Shockley
Road

Ninepin
Branch
Road

Patey
Woods
Road

Mt. Zion Church

Pocomoke
River

Mt. Olive Church

Laws Road

354 (Whiton Road)

12

Old
Furnace
Road

Mt. Olive
Church Road

Old
Trinity
Cemetery

113

Cedartown Road

Furnace
Town

Nassawango Creek
swimming hole

Red House Road

SNOW HILL (see inset
on third page)

Start

394

(continued on
next page)

Taylor
Road

Millville Road

12
(Snow Hill
Road)

365
(Public
Landing
Road)

365

Sand Road

Creek
Road

Nassawango
Road

394

113

12

113

Pocomoke
River

Milburn Landing
State Park

McCabe's
Corner
Road

Pawpaw
Creek
Road

Stagg
Road

© The Countryman Press

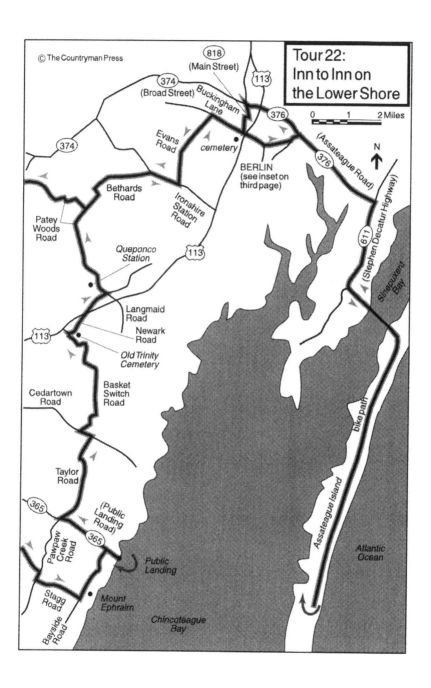

© The Countryman Press

818
(Main Street)

374
(Broad Street)

113

376

Buckingham Lane

Evans Road

cemetery

(Assateague Road)

376

374

BERLIN
(see inset on
third page)

Bethards Road

Ironshire Station Road

Patey Woods Road

611

(Stephen Decatur Highway)

Queponco Station

113

Sinepuxent Bay

Langmaid Road

Newark Road

113

Old Trinity Cemetery

Cedartown Road

Basket Switch Road

Bike path

Taylor Road

365

(Public Landing Road)

Assateague Island

Pawpaw Creek Road

365

Public Landing

Atlantic Ocean

Stagg Road

Mount Ephraim

Bayside Road

Chincoteague Bay

**Tour 22:
Inn to Inn on
the Lower Shore**

0   1   2 Miles

N

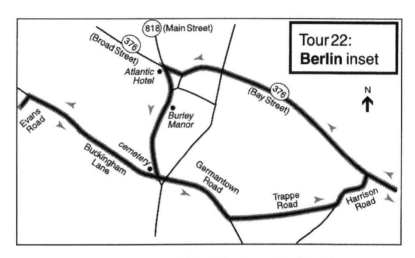

Tour 22:
Berlin inset

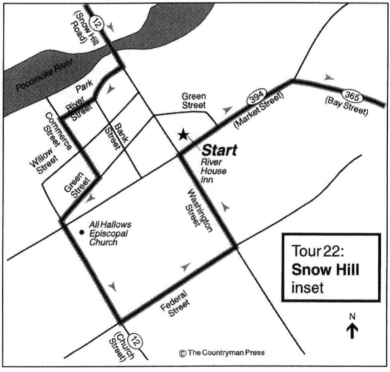

Tour 22:
Snow Hill inset

© The Countryman Press

0.0 *Leaving the River House Inn (or the adjacent municipal parking lot), turn left on Market Street (MD 394).*

The River House, built circa 1860 as a Victorian country home, is set on a green lawn that rolls down to the cypress-dark Pocomoke River. Snow Hill was laid out much earlier, in 1686, and became the county seat in 1742. Since it has no hills and only rarely sees snow, it is assumed that the town was named for the English home of the original tract holder, William Stevens. The early settlers, mainly Scottish Presbyterians from Northern Ireland, wove cloth, manned gristmills, grew tobacco, and carried on commerce with England and with Barbados.

After the Revolution, Baltimore edged out Snow Hill and other colonial ports, and commerce withered. In the early nineteenth century fires devastated the old town, so much of the remaining architecture is Victorian—frame houses with lots of bric-a-brac.

0.1 *Turn right on Bay Street (MD 365), which leads out of town, past a large feed mill and across railroad tracks.*

1.1 *Bay Street crosses US 113 and becomes Public Landing Road.*

2.1 *Turn right on McCabe's Corner Road, which leads through woods and past large chicken farms.*

4.9 *Turn right on Pawpaw Creek Road and then make an immediate left on Stagg Road.*

6.3 *Turn left on Bayside Road, which runs along Chincoteague Bay, source of some of the best oysters in Maryland.*

This region was named Arcadia by Giovanni da Verrazano, who explored the area in 1524.

6.8 *The yellow house at right is Mount Ephraim.*

According to local lore, the inhabitants of this estate staved off a British attack by parading along the shore carrying cornstalks, which, from offshore, gave the appearance of a large military force.

8.0 *Turn right on Public Landing Road to Snow Hill Public Landing, which has a beach and a long pier with gazebos.*

The landing is a great place to sunbathe, swim, or just gaze across Chincoteague Bay, which is about 5 miles wide at this point. In the nineteenth century steamboats landed here and ferried people and goods to Baltimore. Just to the right of the pier is the Spence House, built in stages by a prominent local family in the 1700s and 1800s. It once served as a resort hotel known as the Mansion House.

After a respite, reverse direction and go west on Public Landing Road.

9.6 *Turn right on Taylor Road.*

12.0 *Taylor Road ends. Turn left on Cedartown Road.*

12.3 *Turn right on Basket Switch Road.*

15.8 *Turn right on Newark Road.*

15.9 *To your right, in Old Trinity Cemetery, where graves rest under tall pines, is the Bicentennial Tree.*

A historical marker, placed here in 1976, notes that the tree has stood since before the Revolution. Now, alas, it's just a stump, surrounded by poison ivy.

16.6 *Newark Road crosses US 113 and runs along railroad tracks.*

17.3 *If you need food or a rest room, turn right on Langmaid Road and proceed 0.4 mile to the convenience store/gas station on US 113 (Worcester Highway). (If you don't want to make this detour, turn left at this intersection on Patey Woods Road and deduct 0.8 mile.) After the rest stop, double back on Langmaid Road, which becomes Patey Woods Road after crossing Newark Road.*

18.1 *To your left is Queponco Station, a frame nineteenth-century railroad station.*

20.7 *Turn right on Bethards Road, which travels through farmed fields.*

23.0 *Turn right on Ironshire Station Road.*

23.9 *Turn left on Evans Road, which is unmarked, just before the railroad crossing sign.*

The deserted old house to your right is a familiar sight on the lower Eastern Shore. As farmers become more prosperous, they build modern homes and use the old ones to store crops and tools.

The dunes of Assateague Island form Maryland's easternmost boundary.

26.0 *Turn right on Buckingham Lane.*

27.2 *Buckingham Lane ends at Buckingham Cemetery. Ride through the cemetery, cross Main Street, and continue in the same direction on Germantown Road, which immediately crosses US 113 (Worcester Highway).*

27.8 *Turn left on Trappe Road, which leads past a country church.*

28.6 *Turn left on Harrison Road.*

28.9 *Turn right on Assateague Road (MD 376). This road can be busy on summer weekends, but there is a shoulder.*

31.7 *Turn right on Stephen Decatur Highway (MD 611). Just after the turn, there are several camp stores where you can buy supplies for a picnic on the beach at Assateague.*

35.2 *The highway crosses Sinepuxent Bay on the Verrazano Bridge. The climb up this bridge is the only "hill" on the tour.*

At the top, look left for a view of the skyscrapers of Ocean City. Once you cross the bridge you are on Assateague Island, which has both a state park and a national seashore. The island's only residents are the wild ponies, descendants of horses grazed here by seventeenth-century settlers, plus white-tailed deer, Sitka deer, an Oriental elk introduced during the 1920s, and a wide variety of birds. The ponies are not ponies but horses reduced in size by inbreeding. They live in families consisting of a stallion, several mares, and their offspring. The stallion usually drives the male offspring away, and the outcasts soon start their own families. Signs warn that the ponies bite and kick, and it is illegal to feed them— they thrive on marsh and dune grass. Many of them are quite happy to pose for pictures and can be found in the parking lots and along the roads as well as on the trails that lead to freshwater ponds in the woods. A bicycle path beside the park road leads past beautiful Atlantic beaches, a few historical exhibits, and entrances to several walking trails.

40.1 *The bike path and the road end. Travel beyond this point is either on foot or, with a permit, in a four-wheel-drive vehicle. To continue the tour, double back, recross the Verrazano Bridge, and go north on MD 611.*

48.5 *Turn left on Assateague Road (MD 376), which becomes Bay Street as it enters Berlin.*

52.9 *Bay Street turns into Broad Street. Turn right on Broad Street and proceed about 0.5 block to the Atlantic Hotel at the corner of Broad and Main.*

This restored brick commercial hotel was built in 1895 and is listed on the National Register of Historic Places. It is beautifully furnished with Victorian antiques and offers both formal dining and a pub. The Atlantic Hotel is part of the biking-from-inn-to-inn network.

To continue the trip, turn right from the front of the hotel and go south on Main Street, which is lined with Federal and Victorian homes set back from the road on well-kept lawns.

53.3 *Burley Manor, on your left, is at 313 South Main Street.*

The house was built in the early nineteenth century by descendants of the original owners of a land-grant plantation that once encompassed the whole area. The name Berlin is a corruption of Burley and has nothing Germanic about it.

53.7 *Bear right on the path through Buckingham Cemetery. At the end of the path, turn right on Buckingham Lane.*

54.8 *Turn left on Evans Road.*

56.9 *Evans Road dead-ends. Turn right on Ironshire Station Road.*

57.9 *At the stop sign, bear left on Bethards Road, which leads past chicken farms and cornfields into a shaded wood.*

60.1 *Turn right on Patey Woods Road.*

61.9 *At a V in front of a house, bear left on Ninepin Branch Road, which is unmarked.*

63.2 *At another V, bear right on Whiton Crossing Road.*

64.1 *Whiton Crossing Road lives up to its name by crossing the Pocomoke River, which is very narrow here.*

Pocomoke means "dark waters"—colored by the bark of the cypresses in the swamps that feed it. Designated a Wild and Scenic River, it is the deepest and swiftest tidal river of its width in the United States.

64.7 *Whiton Crossing Road dead-ends in the small settlement of Whiton. Turn left on Whiton Road.*

65.4 *Bear right on Shockley Road.*

66.2 *The graveyard of Mount Zion Church, to your right, holds several Shockleys.*

66.7 *Turn right on Laws Road, which is tree shaded.*

70.0 *At Mount Olive Church, turn left on Mount Olive Church Road, which passes a radio tower and some large farms.*

73.1 *Turn left on Snow Hill Road (MD 12), which is sometimes busy but has a wide shoulder.*

73.7 *Turn right on Old Furnace Road.*

74.8 *To your left is Furnace Town.*

Berlin's restored Atlantic Inn provides food and lodging for cyclists.

Furnace Town contains the restored Nassawango Iron Furnace, Maryland's only bog furnace, and a re-created nineteenth-century town consisting of buildings moved here from other sites in the area (admission fee).

During the 1830s and 1840s, hundreds of people lived and worked on this site, gathering iron ore from nearby bogs, smelting it in the brick-and-stone furnace day and night, and loading the cooled pig iron onto barges to be floated down Nassawango Creek to the Pocomoke River and beyond. The creek also provided power for a sawmill and a gristmill. The surrounding town, called Nescongo, included a post office, school, church, hotel, and a mansion for the ironmaster, as well as smaller homes for the workers. By 1850, higher quality, less expensive iron was available elsewhere, and the entire town was put up for sale. There were no takers, however, and the town simply deteriorated. By the 1970s, when the county historical society took over, all that remained was the tall stack of the iron furnace.

A ramp leads visitors to the top of the stack, where the bog ore was loaded, layered between charcoal and oyster shells. The charcoal in the bottom layer was fired, and hot air was forced through pipes by a bellows powered by a waterwheel. The ore melted and flowed to the bottom, with the oyster shells filtering out impurities.

75.0 *Just past the entrance to Furnace Town, turn left on Millville Road (unmarked), which has Nassawango Creek and a pine-and-holly woods on one side and a cornfield on the other.*

The creek side of the road is a sanctuary owned by the Nature Conservancy.

75.9 *Millville Road ends at the intersection with Sand Road. Bear left on Sand Road.*

76.6 *At the intersection with Red House Road, a slight jog to the left on Red House Road will take you to a pleasant swimming hole on Nassawango Creek. Then continue on Sand Road, which becomes Creek Road.*

78.7 *Turn right on Nassawango Road.*

82.7 Turn left into Milburn Landing State Park and follow the signs to a landing and dock on the Pocomoke River.

84.7 From the landing, retrace your path on Nassawango Road to the intersection with Creek Road. Continue on Nassawango, crossing a wide expanse of lily-pad-covered creek on a bridge.

93.0 Turn left on Snow Hill Road (MD 12) and cross the Pocomoke into Snow Hill.

94.2 Immediately after crossing the bridge, turn right into a river-front park with rest rooms and the landing of Tillie the Tug, an excursion boat that plies the river.

94.3 Turn left on Commerce Street and then right on Green Street.

94.4 Cross Market Street onto Church Street.

On your right stands All Hallows Episcopal Church, built in 1756 in Flemish bond with glazed headers. There were some Victorian renovations, notably a slate roof.

94.6 Turn left on Federal Street.

This street is lined with gracious nineteenth-century homes. The main part of the house at 101 West Federal was built circa 1800 using ship's ballast. Later, the house may have been part of the underground railroad.

94.7 Turn left on Washington Street.

94.9 Turn right on Market Street and return to the River House Inn.

Bicycle Repair Services

A. W. Payne Western Auto, 114 West Green Street, Snow Hill; 410-632-1334
  No rentals
Bike World, 10 Caroline Street, Ocean City; 410-289-2587
  Rentals

156

Accommodations

The River House Inn, 201 East Market Street, Snow Hill, MD 21863;
     410-632-2722
Atlantic Hotel, 2 North Main Street, Berlin, MD 21811; 410-641-3589

For information on Biking Inn-to-Inn on the Eastern Shore, write P.O.
Box 20, Betterton, MD 21610.

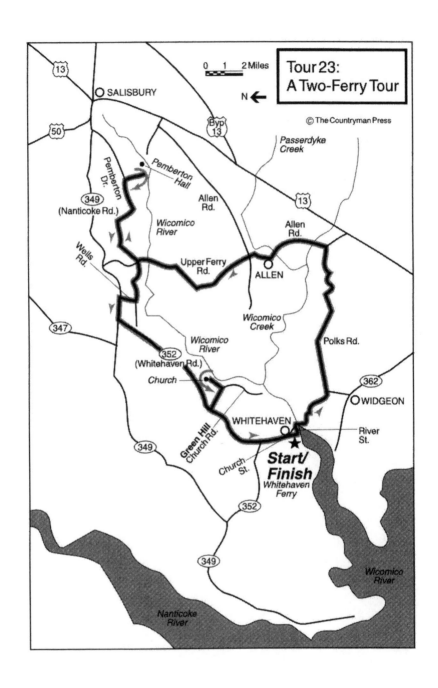

Tour 23:
A Two-Ferry Tour

© The Countryman Press

0 1 2 Miles

N ←

SALISBURY

13

50

349
(Nanticoke Rd.)

Pemberton Dr.

Pemberton Hall

Allen Rd.

Wicomico River

Byp 13

Passerdyke Creek

13

Allen Rd.

Wells Rd.

Upper Ferry Rd.

ALLEN

347

352
(Whitehaven Rd.)

Wicomico River

Church

Wicomico Creek

Polks Rd.

362

WIDGEON

Green Hill Church Rd.

349

WHITEHAVEN

River St.

Start/ Finish

Whitehaven Ferry

Church St.

352

349

Wicomico River

Nanticoke River

23
A Two-Ferry Tour

Location: *Wicomico and Somerset Counties*
Terrain: *Flat*
Road conditions: *Paved country roads*
Distance: *34.7 miles*
Highlights: *Historic Whitehaven, the Whitehaven Ferry, Allen Methodist Church and cemetery, Upper Ferry, Pemberton Hall, Green Hill Episcopal Church*

This flat but scenic Eastern Shore ride begins at the Whitehaven Ferry, which has operated since the 1690s. The cable ferry takes you across the broad, marsh-fringed lower Wicomico River, and the tour continues through farmland, pine forests, and tiny villages that are really only names on the map. After a stop at the historic Allen Methodist Church, built in 1848, the tour recrosses the Wicomico on the Upper Ferry and detours to Pemberton Historic Park for a tour of a restored eighteenth-century plantation. Heading back toward Whitehaven, the tour stops at an eighteenth-century church on the banks of the Wicomico, a small family cemetery, and a restored nineteenth-century schoolhouse.

Whitehaven is near Salisbury. From Baltimore, Washington, or Annapolis, take US 50 across the Bay Bridge and down the Eastern Shore. After you cross the Nanticoke River at Vienna, continue about 8.7 miles and turn right onto MD 347. When MD 347 ends, turn left onto MD 349. In about 0.6 mile, turn right onto MD 352. After about 6.6 miles, MD 352 turns right. You go straight, following Whitehaven Road to the ferry. You'll need to pack a lunch on this tour as there are no restaurants or even stores on the route.

0.0 Board the ferry, which is free, for the short trip across the Wicomico.

Look back at the town, whose buildings are all on the National Register of Historic Places. The town was chartered in 1685 by Col. George Gale, who was the second husband of George Washington's grandmother. The large Victorian building at the ferry landing is a hotel that served passengers on the steamboats that called here regularly until the 1930s. Later, the river was dredged as far up as Salisbury, and Whitehaven changed from a bustling port to a sleepy little village.

After disembarking, continue along the marsh-lined road into a village—really just a crossroads—called Widgeon.

1.5 Turn left onto Polks Road.

6.6 Polks Road ends. Turn left onto Allen Road, which is bordered by cedar and pine woods and chicken farms.

8.6 Allen Road turns right by a picturesque pond and leads through a small settlement.

9.0 On your left is a large graveyard attached to Allen Methodist Church, a landmarked frame country church built in 1848 from lumber logged on-site. Boxwood and cedar grace the cemetery. The church actually faces Collins Wharf Road, but go back to the intersection and follow Allen Road, which turns right and leads past the post office.

9.5 Turn left on Upper Ferry Road

13.6 Recross the Wicomico on the Upper Ferry and continue on Upper Ferry Road.

13.9 Turn right on Pemberton Drive for a detour to historic Pemberton Hall. (If you don't want to see Pemberton Hall, turn left here and follow the directions from mile 22.5.)

Pemberton Drive runs through a neighborhood of posh subdivisions on the outskirts of Salisbury. One of them, New Nithsdale, bears the name of a colonial brick home built in 1735 by Capt. Levin Gale, a planter, trader, and merchant. The house still stands in the midst of the subdivision.

Leaving the landmark village of Whitehaven, the Whitehaven ferry has operated since 1690, and carries passengers across the Wicomico River.

16.4 Follow Pemberton Drive as it turns sharply left.

17.4 Turn right on Plantation Lane into Pemberton Historical Park.

Snatched from the jaws of developers by history-minded citizens, Pemberton Historical Park comprises 250 acres of woods, marshland, hiking trails, outbuildings, and Pemberton Hall. One of the earliest gambrel-roofed houses of the Chesapeake region, Pemberton Hall was built in 1741 by Col. Issac Handy and Ann Dashiell Handy, who camped out on the land for several years before the house was completed. The Handys grew grain, tobacco, and flax here and shipped them from their wharf on the Wicomico. Timbers from the wharf have been dated back to 1746. Archaeological digs, tax inventories, and other research have helped to ensure that the restoration of the house is authentic, down to the original paint colors used in the rooms. (For example, the Prussian blue used in the great room was a status-symbol color since the pigment was not naturally occurring and was, therefore, expensive.) The Flemish-bond brick house, which faces the Wicomico, is typical of the period, gracious but not opulent. Tours are available April through September from 2 to 4 PM Wednesday through Sunday or by appointment. For more information call 410-651-3813 or 410-742-1741.

18.9 Exit Pemberton Historical Park and turn left on Pemberton Drive.

22.5 Cross Upper Ferry Road, continuing on Pemberton Drive.

23.4 Turn left on Wells Road, in an industrial area.

23.9 Turn left onto Nanticoke Road (MD 349), which is busy but has a shoulder.

24.6 Turn left into Whitehaven Road (MD 352), which travels through thick pine and cedar woods.

29.1 Turn left on Green Hill Church Road for a short detour to a historic church. (If you want to skip the church, continue on Whitehaven Road and follow directions from mile 30.9.)

30.0 When Green Hill Church Road turns right, go straight on the grassy lane next to the nursery fields and walk your bike into the church grounds.

The large boxlike brick church replaced a log structure built in 1694. Most of the parishioners of this Episcopal church came by water, and the entrance, with the year 1733 spelled out in glazed headers above the door, faces the Wicomico. The graveyard, sheltered with cedars and pines, contains members of the Dashiell family, relatives of Ann Dashiell Handy of Pemberton Hall.

30.9 *After doubling back on Green Hill Church Road, turn left on Whitehaven Road.*

33.2 *MD 352 turns right. Take Whitehaven Road, which continues straight ahead on a different type of pavement.*

34.3 *At the V, go straight on Church Street, stopping to admire the restored 1886 schoolhouse and to read the historical marker.*

34.7 *Turn left on River Street, which leads back to the ferry or to the Whitehaven Bed & Breakfast.*

Bicycle Repair Services

Salisbury Schwinn/Cycle & Fitness, 1404 South Salisbury Boulevard (US13), Salisbury; 410-546-4747
   Rentals

Accommodations

Whitehaven Bed & Breakfast, 23844–48 River Street, Whitehaven, MD 21856-2506; 410-873-2626

163

WESTERN MARYLAND

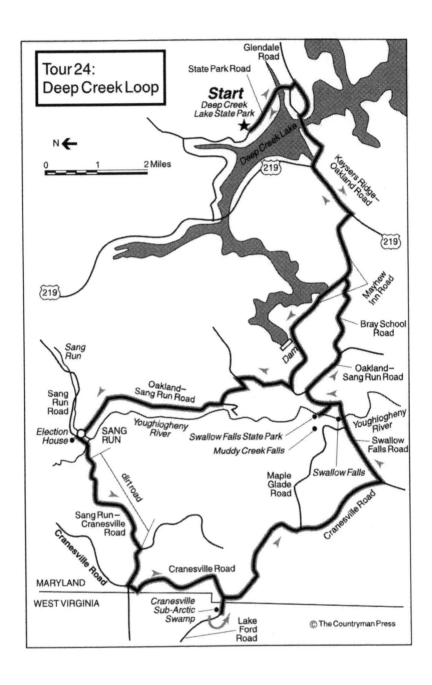

Tour 24:
Deep Creek Loop

Glendale Road
State Park Road
Start
Deep Creek
Lake State Park
Deep Creek Lake
219
Keysers Ridge–Oakland Road
219
N
0   1   2 Miles
219
Mayhew Inn Road
Bray School Road
Sang Run
Dam
Oakland–Sang Run Road
Sang Run Road
Oakland–Sang Run Road
Youghiogheny River
Election House
SANG RUN
Youghiogheny River
Swallow Falls State Park
Muddy Creek Falls
Swallow Falls Road
dirt road
Maple Glade Road
Swallow Falls
Sang Run–Cranesville Road
Cranesville Road
Cranesville Road
MARYLAND
WEST VIRGINIA
Cranesville Road
Cranesville Sub-Arctic Swamp
Lake Ford Road
© The Countryman Press

24
Deep Creek Loop

Location: *Garrett County*
Terrain: *Very hilly*
Road conditions: *Mainly paved light-traffic roads, with a 1-mile stretch on a busy road and one dirt road*
Distance: *33.9 miles*
Highlights: *Deep Creek Lake, the Cranesville Sub-Arctic Swamp, Swallow Falls, Muddy Creek Falls*

The biggest freshwater lake in Maryland, 3,900-acre Deep Creek Lake was created in the 1920s as part of a hydroelectric project. Even before the lake became a recreation mecca, the surrounding area drew outdoors aficionados. In 1918, Henry Ford, Harvey Firestone, and Thomas Edison camped at Muddy Creek Falls. Even earlier, Grover Cleveland, a more sedentary type, honeymooned in nearby Deer Park.

This tour, which is decidedly not for sedentary types, begins in Deep Creek Lake State Park, where you can have a swim before or after the ride. It skirts the lake for a bit, then runs alongside Sang Run and the Youghiogheny River and makes its way over a mountain road to the Cranesville Sub-Arctic Swamp, a nature sanctuary. After stops at two spectacular waterfalls, the tour returns to Deep Creek Lake State Park.

0.0 *Exiting the park, turn left on State Park Road, which leads across a bridge.*

0.3 *As soon as you cross the bridge, turn right on Glendale Road, which crosses another bridge.*

Although it's only 12 miles in length, Deep Creek Lake has a shoreline of 65 miles. Its waters seem to flow into all the nooks and crannies of the land. As a result, riding along the lake means crossing many bridges over narrow sections of water.

A boardwalk leads through the Cranesville Sub-Arctic Swamp,
a relic of an earlier, colder age.

2.3 *Turn left on US 219 (Keysers Ridge–Oakland Road), which can be busy but has a shoulder.*

3.3 *Turn right on Mayhew Inn Road, which has a restaurant on the corner.*

4.0 *The stone barn at your right is in the style characteristic of the area.*

6.4 *To your right is the dam that created the lake.*

7.6 *Turn right on Oakland–Sang Run Road, which runs up and down hills covered with hemlock, laurel, and rhododendron.*

The Youghiogheny River—affectionately known by river rafters as "the Yuck"—can be heard, more often than seen, on your left.

12.9 *Turn left on Sang Run Road, in the small settlement of Sang Run, after stopping for refreshment in Friends Store at the intersection.*

"Sang" is short for ginseng, a medicinal plant prized in Asia as an aphrodisiac. The wild plant once grew in profusion hereabouts and provided income for local farmers.

13.0 *The Election House to your right served as a polling place from 1882 to 1972. Across the road, a park on Sang Run offers picnic tables.*

13.3 *Sang Run Road crosses the Youghiogheny River, passes a farmhouse, bears left, turns to hard-packed dirt, and begins climbing Piney Mountain, following the river on a high ridge.*

To your right, breaks in the forest afford sweeping mountain views.

15.9 *Turn left on Cranesville Road. Ignore the misleading signs to the Cranesville Sub-Arctic Swamp and continue south on Cranesville Road, up a winding hill and past several farms.*

18.1 *Just past a small white church, turn right on Lake Ford Road, which turns to dirt and gravel and leads across the West Virginia line to the swamp, which is owned by the Nature Conservancy.*

Secure your bike in the parking lot and follow signs to the boardwalk built over the swamp, a remnant of the Ice Age. Some plants found in this bog normally grow only in Arctic climes.

18.8 *Exiting the preserve, turn right, continuing south on Cranesville Road.*

23.1 *Make a sharp left onto Swallow Falls Road.*

24.4 *Turn left into Swallow Falls State Park.*

Secure your bike and take a short hike from the parking lot to Swallow Falls and Muddy Creek Falls. Muddy Creek Falls, at 51 feet, is the highest waterfall in Maryland. Henry Ford, Harvey Firestone, and Thomas Edison camped here in 1918 and again in 1921. A photograph now in the Ford Museum in Dearborn, Michigan, shows the pioneer automaker scrubbing his laundry in the creek. Just downstream, Muddy Creek empties into the Youghiogheny River, which quickly tumbles down Swallow Falls, named for the birds that nest in the crevices the river has made in the rocks.

25.3 Exiting the park, turn left on Swallow Falls Road.

25.7 After passing a camp store to your left, Swallow Falls Road winds uphill, lined by tall pines.

26.6 Turn right on Oakland–Sang Run Road.

27.5 Turn left on Bray School Road.

29.2 Turn right on Mayhew Inn Road.

30.6 Turn left on US 219.

31.6 Turn right on Glendale Road and follow it across the bridge.

32.8 Turn left on State Park Road.

33.9 Return to Deep Creek Lake State Park.

Bicycle Repair Services

High Mountain Sports, Route 219, McHenry; 301-387-4199
   Rentals
Rudy's, Wisp Resort, McHenry; 301-387-4640
   Rentals

Accommodations

Garrett County Promotion Council, 200 Third Street, Oakland, MD 21550; 301-334-1948

25

New Germany Jaunt

Location: *Garrett County*
Terrain: *Very hilly*
Road conditions: *Paved country roads*
Distance: *15.5 miles*
Highlights: *New Germany State Park, the National Road, Casselman River Bridge, Penn Alps Restaurant, and artisans' village*

Garrett County played an important part in America's westward push. General Braddock pioneered a military road through here en route to Fort Duquesne—now Pittsburgh—during the French and Indian War. The National Pike—now Alternate US 40—followed. Today, Garrett County's roads are fine for biking, if you don't mind a few hills. Named for John Garrett, a Baltimore & Ohio Railroad official who promoted the area as "America's Switzerland," this is Maryland's highest and westernmost county. Its forested Allegheny Mountain slopes are home to both game and skiers, and its rivers beckon anglers and kayakers.

This tour begins in New Germany State Park, journeys along the National Pike across the Casselman River Bridge into Grantsville, and then follows the Casselman River south, looping back to the park.

0.0 *Exit the state park, which has a swimming lake, boat rental, cabins, campsites, and hiking trails, and head north on New Germany Road. The road cuts through farm country and rolls up and down hills.*

5.1 *After passing over US 40/I-68, turn left on Alt. US 40, the National Pike.*

In the early 1800s, the infant federal government began an ambitious road-building program. The National Pike, which roughly

171

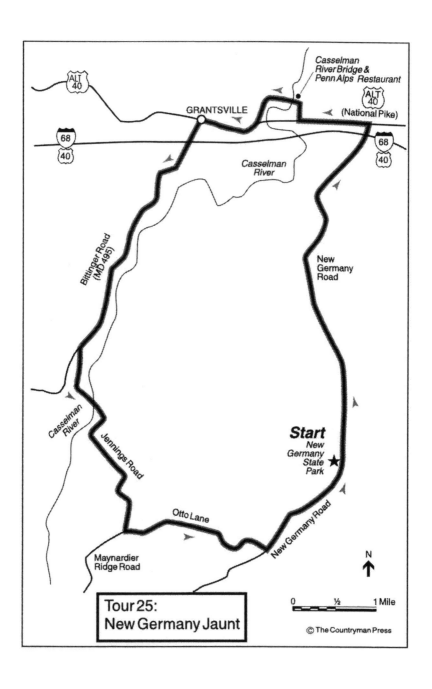

ALT 40

GRANTSVILLE

68
40

Casselman River Bridge &
Penn Alps Restaurant

ALT 40
(National Pike)

68
40

Casselman
River

Bittinger Road
(MD 495)

New
Germany
Road

Casselman
River

Jennings Road

Start
New
Germany
State
Park

Otto Lane

New Germany Road

Maynardier
Ridge Road

N

Tour 25:
New Germany Jaunt

0   ½   1 Mile

© The Countryman Press

followed General Braddock's route, was built as an extension of the Cumberland Road and ran from Cumberland to the Ohio River. Now Alt. US 40, the road carries mainly local traffic, and there is a shoulder.

6.3 *An old mile marker for the National Pike stands at the right.*

6.7 *Bear right at the bottom of the hill to the Casselman River Bridge, which is closed to automobile traffic.*

This single-arch stone bridge, originally constructed in 1813–14 as part of the National Road and restored in 1911, is now part of Casselman River State Park. A steel bridge, built in 1933, carries Alt. US 40 traffic. George Washington crossed the river at this point, known as Little Crossings, while serving as a military aide to General Braddock. When it was constructed, the 89-foot stone span was the largest of its type in America. Reportedly, it was constructed a little longer than necessary in the hope that the planned Chesapeake & Ohio Canal would pass under it, but the canal went only as far west as Cumberland. At the opening ceremony for the bridge, many expressed surprise when the supporting timbers were removed and the bridge did not collapse. The Penn Alps Restaurant, built adjacent to the bridge in 1818 to serve stagecoach passengers, still serves food and drink. Next to the inn are reconstructed log houses and a minivillage where craftspeople demonstrate their skills and sell their wares.

After crossing the stone bridge, bear left and continue west on Alt. US 40.

7.6 *In the center of Grantsville, turn left on Bittinger Road (MD 495), which leads down a long hill and along the Casselman River, to your left.*

10.0 *Bittinger Road crosses the Casselman River and then climbs a hill.*

11.0 *Turn left on Jennings Road, which passes a stone church, crosses a creek, and winds up a long hill.*

13.6 *Turn left on Maynardier Ridge Road, which winds down a long hill with excellent valley views and becomes Otto Lane.*

14.9 *Turn left on New Germany Road.*

15.5 *Reenter New Germany State Park.*

Bicycle Repair Services

High Mountain Sports, Route 219, McHenry; 301-387-4199
  Rentals
Allegany Bike Works, 14419 National Highway, LaVale; 301-729-9708
  Rentals

Accommodations

The Casselman Motor Inn, Main Street, Grantsville, MD 21536; 301-895-5055

Cabins and Campsites

New Germany State Park, Route 2, Grantsville, MD 21536; 301-895-5453

A BONUS TOUR

26

From Mountains to Tidewater
Along the C&O Canal

Location: *Allegany, Washington, Frederick, and Montgomery Counties and the District of Columbia, with forays into West Virginia and Virginia*

Terrain: *Flat on the towpath; some hills on a detour and on routes to restaurants and accommodations*

Road conditions: *Hard-packed dirt towpath, generally in good condition*

Distance: *189 miles (184.5 on the towpath, with added miles for travel to restaurants and lodgings)*

Highlights: *The old Western Maryland Railroad Station, the Paw Paw Tunnel, the Little Orleans store, ruins of the Roundtop Cement Mill, Williamsport and the Cushwa Basin, McMahon's Mill, Shepherdstown, Harpers Ferry, Monocacy Aqueduct, White's Ferry, Leesburg, Great Falls Tavern, houses of canal lockkeepers*

This is a trip through geography and history. The Chesapeake & Ohio Canal, though it doesn't touch the Chesapeake Bay and never made it all the way to Ohio, traverses just about every type of Maryland terrain—from the rugged Allegheny Mountains to the Piedmont Plateau to the beginning of the tidewater area, marked by the initial, tidewater lock at Georgetown. It also spans much of Maryland's—and the country's—history, from the time the young George Washington started a company whose aim was to remove barriers of navigation in order to make the Potomac a passage to the West, to the time—two centuries later—when Supreme Court Justice William O. Douglas led a historic hike to prevent the canal and towpath from being turned into a highway. A trip along the towpath also provides a window on nature, with frequent

At the trail's terminus at milepost 184.5, cyclists survey the map of the C&O Canal.

sightings of deer, raccoons, geese, ducks, beavers, muskrats, turtles, bald eagles, great blue herons, and other wildlife.

Construction on the canal began on July 4, 1828, with great fanfare, with President John Quincy Adams turning the first shovelful of dirt. On the very same day, in Baltimore, another crowd gathered for the ground-breaking of the Baltimore and Ohio Railroad, also headed for the promised land out west. For one reason or another, the railroad reached Cumberland first, by about eight years, making the canal obsolete. From the towpath you can sometimes see the trains whizzing by, a reminder that the railroad personnel used to hoot and jeer at the canal workers with all the superiority of their faster speed.

Since the canal flows downhill—from an elevation of 604 feet at Cumberland to sea level at Georgetown—it makes some sense to start your trip in Cumberland. The Old Western Maryland Railroad Station at Cumberland, which houses a visitors center for the canal, provides an ample and safe parking lot if you want to bring your car. An attractive alternative is the shuttle service from the Washington area or other points provided by Catoctin Bike Tours (1-800-TOUR-CNO). People

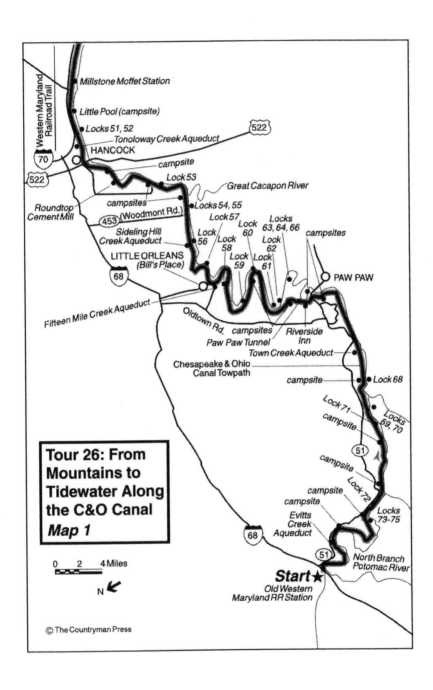

Millstone Moffet Station

Little Pool (campsite)

Locks 51, 52

Tonoloway Creek Aqueduct

522

HANCOCK

Western Maryland Railroad Trail

70

522

campsite

Lock 53

Great Cacapon River

campsites

Locks 54, 55

Roundtop Cement Mill

453 (Woodmont Rd.)

Locks 57

Locks 63, 64, 66

Sideling Hill Creek Aqueduct

Lock 56

Lock 58

Lock 60

Lock 62

campsites

68

LITTLE ORLEANS (Bill's Place)

Lock 59

Lock 61

PAW PAW

Fifteen Mile Creek Aqueduct

Oldtown Rd.

campsites

Riverside Inn

Paw Paw Tunnel

Town Creek Aqueduct

Chesapeake & Ohio Canal Towpath

campsite

Lock 68

Lock 71

Locks 69, 70

campsite

51

campsite

Lock 72

Tour 26: From Mountains to Tidewater Along the C&O Canal
Map 1

campsite

campsite

Evitts Creek Aqueduct

Locks 73-75

68

51

North Branch Potomac River

0   2   4 Miles

N

Start ★
Old Western Maryland RR Station

© The Countryman Press

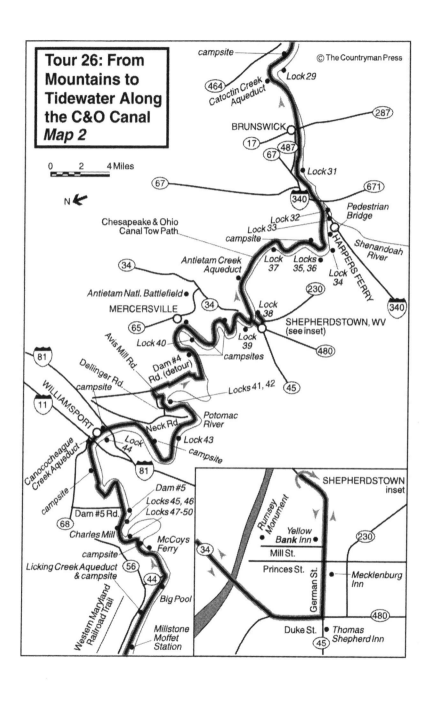

Tour 26: From Mountains to Tidewater Along the C&O Canal *Map 2*

© The Countryman Press

0 2 4 Miles

N

campsite
Lock 29
464 Catoctin Creek Aqueduct
BRUNSWICK
287
17
487
67
Lock 31
67
340
671
Chesapeake & Ohio Canal Tow Path
Lock 32
Lock 33
Pedestrian Bridge
campsite
HARPERS FERRY
Shenandoah River
Antietam Creek Aqueduct
Lock 37
Locks 35, 36
Lock 34
34
Antietam Natl. Battlefield
230
MERCERSVILLE
34
Lock 38
SHEPHERDSTOWN, WV (see inset)
65
Lock 40
Lock 39
480
Avis Mill Rd.
campsites
81
Dellinger Rd.
Dam #4 Rd. (detour)
45
campsite
Locks 41, 42
WILLIAMSPORT
11
Potomac River
Neck Rd.
Lock 44
Lock 43
campsite
81
Canococheague Creek Aqueduct
Dam #5
Locks 45, 46
Locks 47-50
campsite
68
Dam #5 Rd.
Charles Mill
McCoys Ferry
campsite
56
Licking Creek Aqueduct & campsite
44
Western Maryland Railroad Trail
Big Pool
Millstone Moffet Station

SHEPHERDSTOWN inset
Rumsey Monument
Yellow Bank Inn
230
Mill St.
Princes St.
German St.
Mecklenburg Inn
34
Duke St.
Thomas Shepherd Inn
45
480

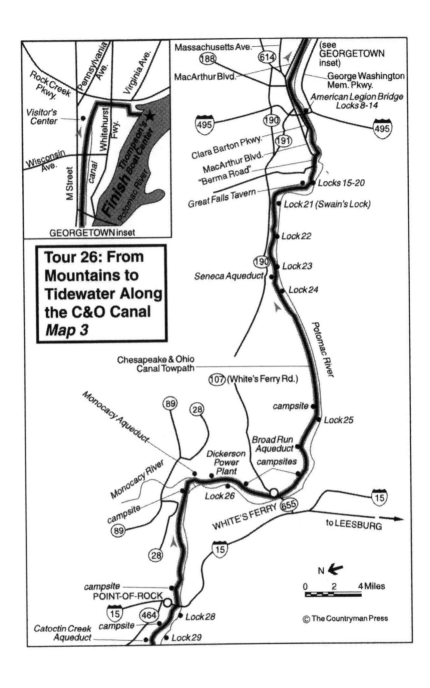

GEORGETOWN inset

Rock Creek Pkwy.
Pennsylvania Ave.
Virginia Ave.
Visitor's Center
Whitehurst Fwy.
canal
Thompson's Boat Center
Finish
Potomac River
Wisconsin Ave.
M Street

Tour 26: From Mountains to Tidewater Along the C&O Canal
Map 3

Massachusetts Ave.
(186)
(614)
(see GEORGETOWN inset)
MacArthur Blvd.
George Washington Mem. Pkwy.
American Legion Bridge
Locks 8-14
(495)
(190)
(495)
(191)
Clara Barton Pkwy.
MacArthur Blvd.
"Berma Road"
Locks 15-20
Great Falls Tavern
Lock 21 (Swain's Lock)
Lock 22
(190)
Lock 23
Seneca Aqueduct
Lock 24
Potomac River

Chesapeake & Ohio Canal Towpath
(107) (White's Ferry Rd.)
campsite
Lock 25
Monocacy Aqueduct
(89)
(28)
Broad Run Aqueduct
Dickerson Power Plant
campsites
Monocacy River
Lock 26
(15)
campsite
(89)
WHITE'S FERRY
(655)
to LEESBURG
(28)
(15)

N ←
0   2   4 Miles

campsite
POINT-OF-ROCK
(15) (464)
Lock 28
Catoctin Creek Aqueduct
campsite
Lock 29

© The Countryman Press

have cycled the canal's 184-mile length in as short a time as two days. This trip, in five days, gives you more time to smell the honeysuckle. It can, of course, be shortened or lengthened.

0.0 *Enter the trail from the railroad-station parking lot and follow it along an embankment through the industrial outskirts of Cumberland. To your right, across a broad meadow, you can see the Potomac River.*

4.2 *Evitts Creek Aqueduct is the westernmost of 11 stone aqueducts built to carry the canal over water. The single-arch structure was built from local stone between 1837 and 1850. Past the aqueduct, the towpath skirts the railroad yards, then veers closer to the Potomac.*

6.9 *A swamp white oak on the right side of the towpath holds a state record for its size. A bench honoring the venerable tree, set against the backdrop of a horse farm, provides a good rest stop.*

9.3 *Lock 75 is the westernmost lock on the canal. Beside it stands the most western-looking, frontierlike lockhouse. It's built of logs and watling, though painted white. These houses came with the lockkeeper's territory, along with a garden where his family could raise, and sometimes sell, produce.*

10.9 *A small exhibit here marks the ruins of a steam pump used to pump river water into the canal. Finished in the late 1970s, the pump could raise 24 cubic feet of water per second. This was needed during periods of drought, or else the canal's water level would sink so low that boat owners would be forced to carry less cargo.*

18.3 *The lock tender's house for Lock 71 has a nice porch for a rest stop. Watch for turtles sunning themselves on logs in the canal, and for water iris and lily pads.*

23.1 *Town Creek Aqueduct, constructed of local limestone, was completed in 1850.*

29.4 *After crossing under a railroad bridge—the railroad crisscrosses the Potomac because the river curves so much—watch for the exit up a slight hill onto MD 51, which will take you*

across the Potomac to Paw Paw, West Virginia, for lunch. Turn right onto MD 51 and cross the bridge into West Virginia. Paw Paw looks like a ghost town, with its once-busy apple warehouses now vacant.

30.3 *The Riverside Inn, a pleasant restaurant with great sandwiches, stands on your left. After lunch, reverse direction and head back across the Potomac into Maryland.*

31.0 *At the C&O Canal sign, turn right toward the canal towpath, following a marked route through a picnic area and some woods to the Paw Paw Tunnel.*

To avoid digging the Chesapeake & Ohio Canal around a 6-mile bend of the Potomac, the engineers decided on a 3,118-foot tunnel right through a mountain that took thousands of workers 14 years to complete. Using a flashlight, walk your bike through the narrow, very dark, and sometimes damp tunnel, built at a cost of about $600,000. Workers, many of them Irish and German immigrants, were paid $10 a month, plus a daily ration of whiskey and meat. They used black gunpowder to blast through the rock and lined the resulting tunnel with five or six layers of bricks. Ethnic feuds plus a cholera epidemic slowed the work.

32.3 *Emerge from the tunnel and continue on the towpath, which makes a straightaway, away from the river, through a hollow. Lavender and pink phlox line the towpath.*

33.4 *At Lock 62, which is lined with wood, the towpath begins to follow the Potomac River.*

46.8 *The towpath crosses Fifteen Mile Creek Aqueduct, a 110-foot stone arch completed between 1848 and 1850. Leave the towpath here and bear left, on a paved road, to the small settlement of Little Orleans.*

This old German settlement became a mini-boomtown during the building of the canal. Many Irish canal workers, some of them victims of a cholera epidemic, are buried at St. Patrick's Catholic Church on the hill above the town. Of more immediate interest is the Orleans Grocery, or Bill's Place, which functions as a camp store, pool hall, bar, and restaurant, and has an inviting porch swing. It was moved from the banks of the river to its present location in 1904 to make room for railroad tracks. If you've made reservations at the Town Hill Hotel, use the phone booth here to call (301-478-2794) for a ride to the hotel, which is 7 miles uphill on Scenic Route 40. The inn is old-fashioned but very comfortable and serves a great breakfast. After breakfast, you and your bikes will be transported back to the towpath to continue the trip.

51.2 *The towpath passes over Sideling Hill Creek Aqueduct and then skirts 1,500-foot Sideling Hill.*

53.8 *At Lock 54, look across to the West Virginia side at the point where the Great Cacapon River enters the Potomac.*

59.0 *The Roundtop Cement Mill, now a ruin, is on your left. Cement from the mill was used to build the Sideling Hill Creek Aqueduct.*

The mill was built here in 1837 to turn newly-discovered local limestone into cement for the canal. It closed in 1909. The stone arches in the rock face held the limestone kilns that were part of the cement operation.

62.3 *Cross the canal on a bridge to Canal Street in Hancock, which parallels the canal, and turn left on Pennsylvania Avenue, where you will find Path Finders, which does bicycle repairs and rents bikes. Continue up Pennsylvania Avenue to Main Street and turn right to Weaver's Restaurant and Bakery, if desired. After your stop, return to the bike shop and turn onto the Western Maryland Railroad Trail, which parallels the towpath but is paved and provides a 10-mile respite from the bumpy towpath.*

66.8 *On your right (your left if you took the towpath rather than the railroad trail) stands Little Pool, a natural pool useful for turning boats around.*

67.7 *A historical marker indicates the site of Millstone Moffet Station on the Western Maryland Railroad and a once-thriving settlement. A pathway to your right leads to a small graveyard, with most of the weathered stones dating from the early 1800s. Watch for poison ivy.*

183

In 1879, a delegation from Hancock came out to meet former President Andrew Jackson here and apologized for the blasts heard from some nearby excavations, asking if they had alarmed Jackson's horse. "My horse and I have heard a similar music before," replied the old soldier.

72.2 *Just short of the end of the paved trail, turn right on an unmarked paved road that leads downhill to the towpath, which rides alongside Big Pool, once a home for canal boats and now home to waterfowl and muskrats.*

76.6 *A historical marker indicates the site of McCoys Ferry, considered a strategic prize during the Civil War.*

In October 1862, Gen. J. E. B. Stuart crossed the Potomac here at the start of a campaign to encircle the Union Army.

78.9 *On your left, across the canal, stand the picturesque ruins of Charles Mill, a gristmill whose grain and flour were loaded onto canal boats.*

The towpath then rounds several cliffs along the river and approaches Dam No. 5, a high-rock dam popular with anglers and a good place to stop and rest. Gen. Stonewall Jackson sabotaged it in 1861, but it was quickly repaired.

84.9 *After crossing Conococheague Creek Aqueduct, take the causeway across the canal into Williamsport.*

Conococheague Creek was an important Indian canoe route. On your right is the Cushwa Basin, one of the busiest wharf areas on the old canal. The old Cushwa warehouse now serves as a canal visitors center. Don't miss the silent film about a canal voyage made in the 1920s.

To go into Williamsport, which has restaurants, a bicycle shop, and a Red Roof Inn, exit the parking lot for the visitors center and go up East Potomac Street. The town is named for Gen. Otho Williams, a Revolutionary War hero. Probably at Williams's behest, George Washington visited here in 1790 to inspect the town as a possible site for the new nation's capital. The town's bid was rejected, partly because of the inability of ships to ascend the Potomac to this point—another impetus for building the canal.

91.4 *Passing through pleasant farmland, the towpath runs along a*

The ruins of the Roundtop Cement Mill, which opened in 1837, stand above the canal its product helped to build.

gravel access road beside a colony of cottages and trailers along the Potomac.

92.0 *The lockkeeper's house for Lock 43 is of whitewashed brick. After Lock 41, the towpath becomes very rough, hugging the shore along some cliffs. Go slowly, or walk your bike.*

The National Park Service has a program to lease some of these houses to people who commit to restoring them. For information about the National Park Service Historic Leasing Program, visit the Web site www.nps.gov/choh.

97.5 *To your left are caverns in the mossy rocks with cold water streaming out of them.*

98.1 *At picturesque red-clapboard McMahons Mill, you need to detour away from the towpath, which is impassable by bicycles for a few miles. Following the signs, turn left at the mill onto Avis Mill Road, which goes up and down hills through rolling farm country.*

98.9 At the T-intersection, turn right on Dellinger Road.

99.3 Turn right on Dam No. 4 Road, which leads along stone fences, past nineteenth-century farmhouses and up and down a series of roller-coaster hills. Keep right at the fork to stay on Dam No. 4 Road and go down a long steep hill toward the river.

102.8 Take a footpath across the canal and rejoin the towpath just below Dam No. 4. The river takes a series of bends after the dam, becoming quite placid, and the towpath passes through some small communities.

106.3 At Taylor's Landing, formerly Mercerville after the first canal company president, a bridge leads across the canal to a seasonal bike and convenience store, Reels and Wheels.

114.7 At Lock 38, exit the parking area and head uphill. Opposite the first house, on your right, you'll see a sign pointing to a shortcut through the woods. (If you don't want to take it, follow the road up the hill to the bridge.) Walk your bike along the path, up a hill, and emerge on the bridge, which leads across the Potomac to Shepherdstown, West Virginia. After crossing the river, continue up a hill and past the Bavarian Inn to the intersection with German Street.

115.7 German Street is the site of interesting shops, historic buildings, a great restaurant in a recycled bank (The Yellow Bank Inn), the Thomas Shepherd Inn, and the Mecklenburg Inn.

The town is also the site of Shepherd College, whose campus includes a vintage child's playhouse, and a river-view park with a monument to James Rumsey (see tour 21), an inventor and engineer who lived here in the late 1700s. From the monument you can look down on the spot where Rumsey demonstrated a working steamboat about 20 years before Robert Fulton's achievement.

After a respite in Shepherdstown, reverse direction, turning right from German Street onto WV 480 and going downhill and across the bridge.

116.4 Turn right into the shortcut and follow the path through the woods. When you emerge onto the road, turn right to the towpath.

119.9 An aqueduct carries the canal over Antietam Creek, downstream from the site of one of the bloodiest battles of the Civil War (see tour 13).

The creek reportedly ran red with blood on September 17, 1862, a day which saw more casualties than any other day in the war, many of them incurred in a fight for a small bridge over Antietam Creek. The graceful structure is made of locally quarried limestone. Look for a small metal disk on the aqueduct bridge, a Geological Survey marker showing the elevation, 120 feet above sea level.

122.4 The lockkeeper for Lock 37 lived in this brick house.

124.3 On the left are ruins of lime kilns that operated into the 1960s.

The adjacent shack was part of a manganese mining operation. Past here, the river begins to be filled with boulders and rapids and is quite wide.

128.5 Look across the river and downstream for a view of Harpers Ferry, West Virginia, and continue to a staircase leading to a footbridge across the Potomac. To cross into this historic town, lock your bike at the rack near the footbridge and take the downstream pedestrian bridge.

The Potomac meets the Shenandoah River here, a sight Thomas Jefferson said was "worth a voyage across the Atlantic." You can view the confluence from Jefferson's vantage point by following the short path to Jefferson's Rock. It also leads to two historic churches that were used as field hospitals during the Civil War; a house where the town's founder, Robert Harper, once lived; and an old cemetery. The town's real moment in history came in 1859 when fiery abolitionist John Brown captured the federal arsenal. The arsenal was recaptured by U.S. Marines under Robert E. Lee two days later, and Brown was captured in the small engine house visible just as you get off the bridge. Much of the town is under the protection of the National Park Service, which offers excellent tours of many of the preserved buildings as well as a bookstore and rest rooms. There are also restaurants here.

After recrossing the pedestrian bridge, turn right and continue on the towpath, which runs between the railroad tracks and the river, which is marked by boulders and rapids.

187

134.2 *Near the remains of Lock 30, you can see the church spires of Brunswick, one of the three largest towns on the canal.*

137.7 *The towpath crosses Catoctin Creek on a new bridge built to replace the crumbling Catoctin Creek Aqueduct, the remaining arch of which can be seen upstream.*

138.3 *The brick lockhouse for Lock 29 has a big, welcoming front porch.*

141.0 *The towpath merges with a paved road in the town of Point-of-Rocks. A small store is accessible if you take the bridge to your left into town. The highlight of the town is its restored Queen Anne–style railroad station, which is on the National Register of Historic Places.*

147.0 *Walk your bike across heavily trussed Monocacy Aqueduct, a seven-arched pink quartzite structure badly in need of repair.*
General Lee ordered the aqueduct destroyed during the Civil War, but the attempt failed. The stone for the aqueduct was quarried at the base of nearby Sugarloaf Mountain.

148.6 *The Dickerson Power Plant looms on both sides of the towpath.*

153.7 *White's Ferry Road crosses the towpath. To take the ferry to Leesburg, Virginia, turn right here.*
The ferry is named for Confederate officer Elijah White, who owned a farm on the Virginia side of the Potomac and guided Confederate troops across the river near here. After the war, White opened a store in Leesburg and, in 1871, started regular ferry service across the Potomac. He named his boat after Gen. Jubal A. Early, who crossed here on his way to raid Washington. The current boat, also called the Jubal Early, is guided by a cable and operates year-round from dawn until past dusk. Unfortunately, the trip into Leesburg involves an unpleasant major highway, although a bike route is planned. However, if you have reservations at the Norris House Inn, the inn will pick you and your bike up on the Virginia side of the river. Call from the pay phone on the Maryland side. Leesburg also has excellent restaurants.

After returning to Maryland on the ferry, follow White's Ferry Road to the towpath and turn right.

The C&O Canal towpath, once slated to be obliterated by a freeway, provides a pathway to history and nature for cyclists and walkers.

158.3 The brick shell of Jarboe's store, one of many that once served canallers, stands on the left.

166.5 Lock 24, called Riley's Lock, is combined in a single structure with Seneca Aqueduct, which carries the canal over Seneca Creek.

After passing below some dramatic cliffs, the towpath meanders through a marshy waterfowl sanctuary.

169.9 Lock 22, or Pennyfield Lock, is made of red Seneca sandstone.

President Grover Cleveland used to stay at the lockhouse here and fish with his friends, the Pennyfields.

170.8 The canal and towpath make a sharp bend and continue beneath some cliffs.

172.8 Swain's Lock has a refreshment stand and picnic tables, and you can rent boats and bikes there.

175.1 At Lock 20 stands the restored Great Falls Tavern, originally Crommelin House, now a National Park Service museum of canal history.

Built in the 1820s and named for a Dutch national who helped float loans for the canal company, the house served both as a residence for the lockkeeper and as a hotel/tavern. Mule-drawn canal boats leave from this point in season, and a walkway leads to a viewing area for the Great Falls of the Potomac.

175.7 Unless you want to carry your bike through the water and across some slippery rocks, take the marked detour that begins here. You have to carry your bike up some stairs to a pedestrian bridge, then turn right along what has become known as "the Berma Road." It ends in the parking lot across MacArthur Boulevard from The Old Anglers Inn, a posh and excellent restaurant that serves meals on its terrace. To continue on the towpath from The Old Anglers Inn, go across the parking lot to a causeway that leads to the towpath. Turn left.

180.1 Pass under the American Legion Bridge, which carries the Capital Beltway across the Potomac. You will then ride by four locks in rapid succession.

183.1 On your right is the private Sycamore Island Club, accessible to members by a rope-guided ferry.

185.4 Ride either on the wooden walkway or, if the water isn't too deep, on the concrete spillway.

186.1 Fletcher's Boathouse (right) sells refreshments and rents canoes and rowboats.

Across the canal lies the Abner Cloud House, one of the oldest buildings on the canal, built in 1801. Cloud stored grain and flour from his nearby mill in the basement. The paved Capital Crescent Trail parallels the towpath at this point and provides an alternative route into Georgetown.

187.6 In the river lie the Three Sisters Islands.

These rocky islets were once supposed to be under a proposed new bridge to Virginia. Conservationists foiled the attempt. Look downriver for views of the Watergate and the Kennedy Center. As you enter Georgetown, the towpath makes several bridge crossings and, in places, is paved with cobblestones. Heavy pedestrian traffic means you should probably walk your bike.

188.9 A bronze bust of Supreme Court Justice William O. Douglas commemorates the successful fight to prevent the canal and towpath from being paved over for a road.

Canal boats leave from this point in season.

189.0 The towpath ends on Rock Creek Parkway, near Thompson's Boat Center at the intersection with Virginia Avenue.

The actual canal continues to a tidelock, where Rock Creek flows into the Potomac on the grounds of Thompson's Boat Center. To reach the Foggy Bottom Metro station, turn left on Virginia Avenue and left again on New Hampshire Avenue.

Bicycle Repair Service

Cycles & Things, 165 North Centre Street, Cumberland; 301-722-5496
No rentals

Path Finders, 6 South Pennsylvania Avenue, Hancock; 301-678-6870
Rentals

Potomac Pushbikes, 11 East Potomac Street, Williamsport; 301-582-4747
Rentals

Reels and Wheels, 17328 Taylors Landing Road, Sharpsburg; 301-432-7281
March through November; no rentals

Bicycle Outfitters, 19 Catoctin Circle NE, Leesburg, VA; 703-777-6126
Rentals

Big Wheel Bikes, 1034 33rd Street NW, Washington, DC; 202-337-0254
Rentals

Accommodations

Inn at Walnut Bottom, 127 Greene Street, Cumberland, MD 21502; 301-777-0003

Paw Paw Patch B&B, P.O. Box 291, Paw Paw, WV 25434; 304-947-7496

Town Hill Hotel B&B, Scenic Route 40, Little Orleans, MD 21766; 301-478-2794

Cohill Manor B&B, 5102 Western Pike, Hancock, MD 21750; 301-678-7573

Red Roof Inn, 310 East Potomac Street, Williamsport, MD 21795; 301-582-3500

Yellow Brick Inn & Restaurant, 201 East German Street, Shepherdstown, WV 25443; 304-876-2208

Thomas Shepherd Inn, 300 West German Street, Shepherdstown, WV 25443; 304-876-3715

Mecklenburg Inn, 128 East German Street, Shepherdstown, WV 25443; 304-876-2126

Hilltop House Hotel, 400 East Ridge Street, Harpers Ferry, WV 25425; 304-535-2132

Norris House Inn, 108 Loudon Street, Leesburg, VA 22075; 1-800-644-1806

In addition, the Norris House Inn publishes a planner listing B&Bs convenient to the towpath and other bicycle paths. For more information visit the inn's Web site, http://norrishouse.com.

94041489R00108

Made in the USA
Middletown, DE
17 October 2018